Monsen and Baer, Inc. - Box 529 Vienna, VA 22183 USA (703) 938-2129 FAX: (703) 242-1357

ACTUAL PRICES REALIZED: THE MYSTIQUE OF PERFUME email: monsenbaer@erols.com

Monsen and Baer Perfume Bottle Auction XVII - May 4, 2007. Atlanta, Georgia.

The prices listed include the 15% buyer's commission.

Omitted lot numbers represent lots which were unsold or withdrawn as of the publication of this list.

LOT #	PRICE	LOT #	PRICE	LOT #	PRICE	LOT #	PRICE	LOT #	PRICE
1.	$46.00.	91.	$138.00.	175.	$92.00.	279.	$460.00.	366.	$373.75.
2.	$46.00.	92.	$299.00.	176.	$115.00.	280.	$1,840.00.	369.	$1,150.00.
3.	$23.00.	94.	$103.50.	177.	$69.00.	282.	$805.00.	370.	$1,725.00.
4.	$46.00.	95.	$161.00.	178.	$115.00.	283.	$1,610.00.	377.	$69.00.
5.	$57.50.	96.	$287.50.	179.	$149.50.	288.	$195.50.	381.	$195.50.
6.	$34.50.	99.	$115.00.	180.	$149.50.	289.	$115.00.	384.	$2,300.00.
7.	$69.00.	102.	$57.50.	182.	$46.00.	290.	$172.50.	385.	$1,610.00.
8.	$69.00.	103.	$241.50.	183.	$172.50.	291.	$253.00.	389.	$632.50.
11.	$34.50.	104.	$34.50.	186.	$402.50.	292.	$195.50.	391.	$920.00.
12.	$23.00.	105.	$218.50.	187.	$23.00.	293.	$115.00.	392.	$1,840.00.
13.	$161.00.	106.	$218.50.	188.	$103.50.	294.	$57.50.	393.	$1,380.00.
16.	$46.00.	107.	$161.00.	191.	$46.00.	295.	$92.00.	395.	$3,450.00.
17.	$126.50.	108.	$230.00.	192.	$184.00.	296.	$126.50.	396.	$2,127.50.
18.	$34.50.	109.	$126.50.	193.	$126.50.	299.	$69.00.	397.	$862.50.
19.	$34.50.	110.	$57.50.	195.	$161.00.	301.	$184.00.	399.	$115.00.
23.	$46.00.	113.	$373.75.	196.	$57.50.	303.	$103.50.	402.	$1,150.00.
24.	$23.00.	114.	$57.50.	197.	$46.00.	304.	$172.50.	407.	$2,300.00.
25.	$69.00.	116.	$977.50.	198.	$34.50.	305.	$126.50.	408.	$1,150.00.
26.	$172.50.	117.	$92.00.	199.	$103.50.	306.	$218.50.	412.	$488.75.
27.	$138.00.	120.	$207.00.	201.	$1035.00.	307.	$149.50.	414.	$4,025.00.
28.	$34.50.	121.	$345.00.	203.	$632.50.	309.	$207.00.	416.	$575.00.
32.	$57.50.	122.	$345.00.	205.	$287.50.	310.	$138.00.	417.	$2,990.00.
33.	$34.50.	123.	$488.75.	206.	$230.00.	312.	$805.00.	418.	$3,737.50.
34.	$172.50.	125.	$5,175.00.	207.	$34.50.	313.	$373.75.		
35.	$103.50.	127.	$4,887.50.	209.	$172.50.	316.	$115.00.	Want to be on	
37.	$69.00.	128.	$103.50.	213.	$115.00.	317.	$126.50.	our Mailing List?	
38.	$103.50.	129.	$46.00.	215.	$172.50.	318.	$172.50.	Just call or write.	
39.	$172.50.	130.	$264.50.	217.	$80.50.	319.	$322.00.	Next Auction:	
40	$57.50.	134.	$1,265.00.	219.	$195.50.	320.	$80.50.	May 2, 2008.	
41.	$241.50.	135.	$6,900.00.	221.	$632.50.	321.	$103.50.	St Louis, Missouri.	
43.	$161.00.	136.	$23.00.	222.	$172.50.	322.	$218.50.		
44.	$115.00.	137.	$34.50.	232.	$195.50.	323.	$80.50.		
45.	$345.00.	140.	$1,150.00.	233.	$241.50.	326.	$310.50.		
47.	$57.50.	141.	$126.50.	236.	$299.00.	327.	$207.00.		
49.	$241.50.	142.	$488.75.	237.	$92.00.	328.	$92.00.		
50.	$115.00.	144.	$1,150.00.	238.	$57.50.	331.	$517.50.		
52.	$172.50.	146.	$2,300.00.	240.	$115.00.	332.	$207.00.		
54.	$1955.00.	147.	$977.50.	241.	$11.50.	333.	$126.50.		
56.	$431.25.	148.	$69.00.	243.	$230.00.	334.	$115.00.		
60.	$1,035.00.	149.	$1,495.00.	250.	$345.00.	335.	$322.00.		
65.	$184.00.	150.	$431.25.	252.	$575.00.	337.	$488.75.		
68.	$103.50.	151.	$575.00.	253.	$230.00.	340.	$69.00.		
69.	$690.00.	154.	$172.50.	254.	$632.50.	343.	$373.75.		
70.	$103.50.	157.	$92.00.	255.	$207.00.	344.	$184.00.		
71.	$92.00.	159.	$23.00.	257.	$977.50.	346.	$805.00.		
72.	$80.50.	162.	$57.50.	258.	$253.00.	351.	$103.50.		
73.	$431.25.	163.	$126.50.	259.	$103.50.	352.	$138.00.		
77.	$34.50.	164.	$57.50.	260.	$1,725.00.	353.	$402.50.		
78.	$57.50.	165.	$34.50.	262.	$6,900.00.	354.	$805.00.		
79.	$57.50.	166.	$230.00.	264.	$402.50.	356.	$402.50.		
80.	$80.50.	167.	$46.00.	269.	$460.00.	357.	$2,300.00.		
81.	$46.00.	168.	$184.00.	270.	$517.50.	358.	$747.50.		
82.	$230.00.	169.	$23.00.	271.	$241.50.	359.	$690.00.		
84.	$34.50.	170.	$80.50.	272.	$195.50.	361.	$690.00.		
85.	$92.00.	172.	$115.00.	273.	$184.00.	363.	$1,495.00.		
89.	$431.25.	173.	$149.50.	276.	$2,185.00.	364.	$230.00.		
90.	$287.50.	174.	$92.00.	277.	$546.25.	365.	$1,380.00.		

For Karene Tupp

Rundall B. Mann

Rod Baer

MONSEN AND BAER, Inc.

The Mystique of Perfume

Perfume Bottle Auction XVII

May 4, 2007.

Auctioneer: Michael DeFina

Auction: Crowne Plaza Ravinia Hotel
4355 Ashford Dunwoody Road - Atlanta, Georgia 30346 USA

Auction Preview: All lots will be available for viewing
and inspection from 10:00 AM to 5:00 PM on Friday, May 4, 2007.
Sale will begin at 5:00 PM, May 4, 2007.

**Monsen and Baer, Inc.
Box 529
Vienna, VA 22183 USA
(703) 938-2129 Fax (703) 242-1357
email: monsenbaer@erols.com**

ISBN# 1-928655-07-6

The Mystique of Perfume

Table of Contents

MONSEN AND BAER PERFUME BOTTLE AUCTION SEVENTEEN

Preface

To our fellow collectors in this country and abroad, greetings and good wishes! This is the seventeenth fully catalogued auction of perfume bottles produced by Monsen and Baer. This auction serves to support the International Perfume Bottle Association in that it is held during the annual IPBA Convention, and that a portion of the proceeds of the auction will be accorded to that organization. If you are a serious collector of perfume bottles, you should become a member of the IPBA, the International Perfume Bottle Association. Randall Monsen is a past president of the IPBA, and Rod Baer has served two terms as Publications Chair. The IPBA publishes a wonderful *Perfume Bottle Quarterly,* a Membership Directory, and organizes an outstanding annual Convention. We will happily send membership information and a sample of the *Perfume Bottle Quarterly* to all who request it.

The Mystique of Perfume follows upon the success of our previous books, beginning with *The Beauty of Perfume* in 1996 and following our 2006 book, *The Allure of Perfume.* As in all our previous books, we have tried to give our readers a valuable resource for perfume bottle collecting. Over the last seventeen years, Monsen and Baer publications have given collectors dozens of valuable research articles on the history of perfume companies and glass makers, in addition to photos and descriptions of thousands of perfume bottles.

The Mystique of Perfume offers collectors an astonishing array of perfume bottles, including a wonderful array of rarities of the commercial type, particularly in the categories of Baccarat and Lalique. The auction will finish with a tour de force of Czechoslovakian bottles.

Our overall goal in publishing books on perfume bottles is to provide the collector with a resource for collecting and research that can be used over and over again, not only on the documentation of perfume bottles and their current value, but also on their history and their makers. The hardcover book format provides a durable object for collectors to use and re-use. Our goal here goes beyond merely selling perfume bottles, though of course we wish to do that and to do it well. In a very real sense, we want to produce for collectors something that we, as collectors ourselves, would value and find useful—something we would want to own and keep on our bookshelf. Our sincere wish is that other collectors use it, learn from it, and enjoy it. What we have said in the past bears repeating here: *Knowledge–and the sharing of it–enhances the pleasure of collecting.*

We have both been collectors since early childhood—collectors of many disparate things, not just perfume bottles. A current passion for both of us is American art pottery, in particular the Roseville Pottery and other potteries of Ohio. We have spent a lot of time thinking about the art of collecting. Why do we collect? How can we have more enjoyment collecting? What advice should we give to new collectors? Collecting is an art which has as its first rule that there are no absolute rules. Each collector must decide for herself or himself what to collect and how to go about collecting it. It follows that there are as many different collections as there are collectors. Some collectors collect only commercial perfumes, some only those that are not commercial, some collect miniature perfumes, some only the larger ones. Some collect only a very specific type and others collect anything they find that gives them pleasure. Nonetheless, it seems wise to us to recommend something to our fellow collectors. *First, buy books. Spend some of the collecting budget on books.* An investment in knowledge is always worthwhile, and generally the book will pay for itself in short time. Books will help one to identify objects that definitely should be acquired and others that may be passed. Books will help one avoid mistakes. But probably most important is this: knowledge increases one's pleasure, and if collecting is not about pleasure it is about nothing at all. A second piece of advice for collectors is to build quality into the collection, regardless of what type of collection it is. *Quality is more important than quantity—vastly more important.* Building quality into a collection means selecting objects of known quality and paying a fair price for them. We believe that as the twenty-first century unfolds, collectors will look back longingly and wistfully upon this sale as an opportunity to acquire incredibly desirable perfume bottles at advantageous prices. Our hope is that each collector of today will also recognize this opportunity to acquire a wonderful perfume bottle for their collection.

If you have a truly special perfume bottle that you would consider selling, then our year 2008 auction may be the perfect venue to do so. Monsen and Baer can showcase your bottle in a book which becomes a permanent part of the literature on perfume bottles, and which can then be seen by everyone for decades to come. We also purchase bottles and sometimes entire collections directly, for those who prefer an immediate sale. For those who would like to consign bottles for the year 2008 auction, please contact us *soon after this sale.* Consignment details will be sent to those who request this information. The consignment deadline is November 30, 2007, but many categories fill up *long* before that date.

The collecting of perfume bottles has enriched our lives immeasurably. First, there is the excitement of discovering and purchasing each new bottle. Then there is the joy of seeing, holding, and owning these beautiful objects, a joy that never weakens or grows old. We even enjoy selling some of them, and seeing what pleasure they will give to another collector. And in addition to all this, there are many personal relationships we have developed through this wonderful hobby, and maybe that is the greatest benefit. Thus, collecting perfume bottles has given us much, and we wish in turn to strengthen and enrich this pleasureful pastime. When we began the Monsen and Baer perfume bottle auction seventeen years ago, we had little idea where it would lead us, or of the vast amount of work that would eventually be required to produce a hard-cover book such as *The Mystique of Perfume.* But this journey has been worthwhile, and we have grown to meet the challenges of each new year. We will continue to try to improve our publications as well as the quality of the bottles we offer for sale. We want everyone to know that we have written this book with great joy, and we sincerely hope that it will also bring enjoyment, knowledge, and a deepened appreciation of this wonderful collecting field to our fellow collectors. *To each of our readers: may your collections grow in quality, and may there be no limit to the pleasure you derive. Enjoy!*

Randy Monsen

Rod Baer

The Conditions of Sale
All lots sold in this auction are subject to the following conditions: please read carefully.

Terms of Sale. All lots will be sold, in the numerical sequence of this catalogue, to the highest bidder as determined by the auctioneer. In the case of disputed bids, the auctioneer shall have the sole discretion of determining the purchaser, and may elect to reoffer the lot for sale. We will accept cash, travelers checks, or personal checks with acceptable identification or if the buyer is known to us; we reserve the right in some cases to ship the lot to the purchaser after their check has cleared. Credit card sales are welcome.

Sales Tax. **All lots are subject to Georgia state sales tax unless a valid tax exemption form has been filed with us; proof of sales tax exemption status may be required, i.e., a xerox copy of your sales tax registration form.**

Absentee Bids. A form for absentee bids is available. We will be happy to execute your bid for you as if you were present at the auction. When you do this, it does not mean that the bidding will commence with your bid, it simply means that we will not bid for you above the amount you indicate. It is advantageous to place these absentee bids as early as possible. In the case of identical bids, the bid from the floor will take precedence; for identical absentee bids, the earlier-dated bid will take precedence. Please read shipping information below. **Telephone Bids:** A very limited number of telephone lines may be available for telephone bidding. There is a $50 non-refundable fee for telephone bidding, which must be arranged two weeks prior to the auction--no exceptions.

Bidding Increments. Bidding increments are totally at the discretion of the auctioneer. However, the following increments are typically used: under $50, increments of $5; $50-$300, increments of $10; $300-$500, increments of $25; $500-$1,000, increments of $50; $1,000-$3,000, increments of $100; $3,000-$5,000, increments of $250; $5,000-$10,000, increments of $500; above $10,000, increments of $1,000.

Shipping and Handling Fees. We offer the possibility of shipping your purchases. For the United States and Canada, the flat charge for this service is **$15 per lot** for lots whose sale price is less than $1000; the charges will be higher for the lots valued over $1000 due to insurance charges. Lots which consist of large items can be shipped, with actual shipping charges to be paid by the purchaser.

Shipping purchases to Europe is also possible. **There is an initial charge of $75 for this service; additional lots will be included at the actual shipping cost, which may go above that amount if several lots are purchased.** Absentee bidders will be sent an invoice for the shipping charges and balance due; we offer the convenience of accepting payment in all major European currencies. We normally use United Parcel Service or DHL to ship to Europe, and in most cases we cannot use the Postal Service. United Parcel Service is highly reliable and extremely rapid. However, please note that the minimum charge for a small parcel sent by UPS to Europe is $75. Parcels consisting of several lots may cost twice that amount. Lots which are shipped outside the United States are subject to customs duties in the destination country, which is based upon the purchase price of the lot and we are required to state it. It is the responsibility of the purchaser to determine the amount of these duties and to pay them in full.

Price Estimates and Reserves. Some lots are offered for sale with a "reserve price." The reserve is a confidential minimum price below which the lot will not be sold. The reserve price for any lot in this sale is usually well below the low estimate and is never allowed to be higher than the estimates. The estimates are merely a range within which we believe the lot may find a buyer, but of course many lots may be sold at prices well below or well above these estimates, depending on the wishes of the bidders.

Buyer's Premium. A buyer's premium of **15%** will be added to the hammer price of all lots, to be paid by the buyer as a part of the purchase price.

Condition of Lots. While we attempt to describe the condition of each lot as accurately as possible, as in all auctions, the lots here are sold "as is." We attempt to mention in the descriptions any negative aspect we think bidders need to know, for example: [label absent], [chip to stopper], etc. However, many factors relating to condition cannot be adequately described in the short captions of this catalogue, and this is especially true in the case of miniature or group lots. Very many perfume bottles have exceedingly tiny chips around the opening where the stopper enters the bottle. Sometimes these may also be found on the tongue of the stopper or on the base of the bottle. The boxes and labels of commercial bottles all show varying signs of usage and age, such as discoloration and fraying, and unless we note that the box is in pristine condition, such signs of age should be expected. All bottles, and especially commercial ones, may contain perfume residue and other internal stains. Not all stoppers fit into the bottle with perfect snugness and symmetry, especially those of Czechoslovakian manufacture. Therefore, bidders should inspect each lot they wish to bid on prior to purchase. We would also be happy to discuss the condition of any lot prior to the sale. Unless stated otherwise, the bottles are empty of perfume.

Note on the sizes of bottles: The photographs in this catalogue depict the lots as clearly as possible. However, most photographs show the bottles *smaller* than they actually are, and some photos, especially the full page portraits, may show the bottles *larger* than they actually are. Read the lot descriptions to know the actual sizes. Measurements given in this catalogue are in inches and centimeters, rounded in most cases to the nearest quarter inch or half-centimeter.

In cases where glass by a particular maker is described as unsigned, the catalogue can only provide a reasonable surmise, not a guarantee, as to the maker. Many of the early French glass makers produced glass of similar quality and design. In these cases, the buyer should consult the available reference works and thereafter make their own determination. The glass made by Lalique & Cie. is all grouped together; this includes bottles designed after René Lalique's death by Marc and Marie Claude Lalique. Following the convention used in Utt [1990], perfume bottles produced for sale by R. Lalique & Cie. are referred to as Maison Lalique or Cristal Lalique.

Reference numbers are provided for Lalique, Baccarat, and in many cases for Czech glass and commercial bottles, as described in Utt [1990], Compagnie des Cristalleries de Baccarat [1986], North [1990], Forsythe I & II [1982 & 1993], Lefkowith [1994], and Leach [1997]. These reference numbers are used throughout the catalogue.

Consignments. We will be accepting consignments for our eighteenth auction, to be held May 2008, and we are particularly in search of fine perfume bottles. Our rates of consignment are very competitive with other auctions, and we can offer exposure of your bottles to a specialized buying audience. We guarantee confidentiality. We also purchase individual bottles or entire collections outright, if that avenue of sale is preferred. Contact us and we would be happy to discuss these terms with you. We are especially interested in perfume bottles of high quality, not broken or damaged pieces. Please bear in mind that consignments for the year 2008 auction must be completed by November 30, 2007 to allow sufficient time to prepare and publish the catalogue; many categories fill up well before that date.

Bibliography on the Collection of Perfume

L'Argus des Ventes aux Enchères Valentine's: Verrerie. Paris: Dorotheum Editions, 2000.
Atlas, M. and Monniot, A. *Guerlain - Les Flacons à Parfum Depuis 1828.* Toulouse, France: Editions Milan, 1997.
Atlas, M. and Monniot, A. *Un Siècle d'Echantillons Guerlain.* Toulouse, France: Editions Milan, 1995.
Ball, J. D. and Torem, D. H. *Commercial Fragrance Bottles.* Atglen, Pennsylvania: Schiffer Publishing Co., 1993.
Ball, J. D. and Torem, D. H. *Fragrance Bottle Masterpieces.* Atglen, Pennsylvania: Schiffer Publishing Co., 1996.
Barlow, Raymond E., and Kaiser, Joan E. *A Guide to Sandwich Glass: Vases, Colognes, and Stoppers.* West Chester, Pa: Schiffer Publishing, 1987.
Barille, Elisabeth. *Coty.* Paris: Editions Assouline, 1995.
Berger, C. & D. *Tous les Parfums du Monde.* Toulouse: Editions Milan, 1995.
Bonduelle, J. P. et Lancry, J. M. *Flacons à Parfums Catalogues pour les Ventes aux Enchères Publiques.* March 31, 1990; March 24, 1991; June 16, 1991; October 24, 1991; June 21, 1992; May 16, 1993; November 21, 1993; March 27, 1994; November 20, 1994; June 18, 1995; December 3, 1995; June 16, 1996; December 1, 1996; June 15, 1997; December 7, 1997; November 25, 2000; expert: J.-M. Martin-Hattemberg.
Bonhams *Scent Bottle and Lalique auction catalogues.* November 29, 1989; October 18, 1990; November 21, 1990; April 24, 1991; October 24, 1991; October 28, 1991; April 28, 1992; October 29, 1992; April 7, 1993; June 28, 1993; October 20, 1993; expert: Juliette Bogaers; September 29, 1997; experts Isobel Muston, Eric Knowles, and Emma Thommeret.
Bowman, Glinda. *Miniature Perfume Bottles.* Atglen, Pennsylvania: Schiffer, 1994.
Brine, Lynda and Whitaker, Nancy. *Scent Bottles Through the Ages: An A - Z Pictorial* Bath, UK: Brine and Whitaker, 1998.
Byrd, Joan. *DeVilbiss Perfumizers & Perfume Lights: The Harvey K. Littleton Collection.* Cullowhee, North Carolina: Western Carolina University, 1985.
Cabré, M., Sebbag, M., Vidal, V.. *Femmes de Papier - Perfumed Cards.* Toulouse: Editions Milan, 1998.
Cabré, Monique. *La Légende du Chevalier d'Orsay: Parfums de Dandy.* Toulouse: Editions Milan, 1997.
Camard. Prestige de la Parfumerie. Paris, June 5, 2003. Expert: J.-M. Marti-Hattemberg.
Charles-Roux, Edmonde. *Chanel and Her World.* New York: Vendome Press, 1981.
Chassaing, Rivet, Fournié. *Flacons à Parfums Catalogue pour la Vente aux Enchères Publiques.* June 27, 1994, Toulouse, France; expert: Geneviève Fontan.
Christie's South Kensington. *Lalique including the Pickard-Cambridge Collection of Lalique Scent Bottles,* May 12, 2000.
Christin, Jean. *Flacons à parfum du XXe siècle.* September 29, 1996, Hotel des Bergues, Geneva, Switzerland.
Clements, M. L. and Clements, P. R. *Avon Collectible Fashion Jewelry and Awards.* Atglen, PA: Schiffer & Co., 1998.
Cohet et Feraud *Floréal Perfume Bottle Auction Catalogue,* Toulouse, France, April 15-16, 1995; November 4, 1995; expert: Flora Entajan.
Colard, Grégoire. *[Caron] The Secret Charm of a Perfumed House.* Paris: J. C. Lattès, 1984.
Compagnie des Cristalleries de Baccarat. *Baccarat Les Flacons à Parfum/The Perfume Bottles.* Paris: Henri Addor & Associés, 1986.
Courset, J-M. *5000 Miniatures de Parfum.* Toulouse: Editions Milan, 1995.
Courset, J-M, and Dekindt, P.. *6000 Miniatures de Parfum.* Toulouse: Editions Milan, 1998.
Coutau-Bégarie, O. *Flacons à Parfums Catalogues pour les Ventes aux Enchères Publiques.* December 6, 1993; October 24, 1994; June 12, 1995; November 27, 1995; June 3, 1996; December 1, 1997; November 16, 1998; June 7, 1999; April 17, 2000; November 6, 2000; November 18, 2002; March 29, 2004; expert: Régine de Robien; May 26, 2005, expert: Betty de Stefano.
Demornex, Jacqueline. *Lancôme.* Paris: Editions du Regard, 1985.
Doyle New York. *Belle Epoque sales of February 7, 2001; June 6, 2001.* Expert: Eric Silver
Drouot-Richelieu, Neret-Minet, Coutau-Begarie. *Flacons à Parfums Catalogues pour les Ventes aux Enchères Publiques.* June 23, 1986; April 2, 1987; Nov. 4, 1987; April 13, 1988; Nov. 7, 1988; May 20, 1989; Nov. 13, 1989; May 21, 1990; Nov. 24, 1990; April 8, 1991; May 27, 1991; Nov. 15, 1991; December 14, 1992; expert: Régine de Robien.
Drouot-Richelieu, Neret-Minet. *Flacons à Parfums Catalogue pour la Vente aux Enchères Publiques.* December 14, 1992; expert: J.-M. Martin-Hattemberg.
Drouot-Richelieu, Millon & Robert. *Flacons à Parfums: Catalogue pour la Vente aux Enchères Publiques.* December 6, 1991; expert: Régine de Robien.
Duchesne, Clarence, ed. *La Mémoire des Parfums,* Numeros 1-11. Paris, 1988-1991.
Duval, René. *Parfums de Volnay.* Catalogue of the Company, 1928.
Edwards, Michael. *Fragrances of the World 2000; Fragrances of the World 2001.* Sydney, Australia: Michael Edwards, 2000 and 2001.
Edwards, Michael. *The Fragrance Adviser 1999.* Sydney, Australia: Michael Edwards, 1999.
Edwards, Michael. *Perfume Legends: French Feminine Fragrances.* Sydney, Australia: HM Editions, 1996.
Enghien. *Flacons de Parfum.* June 22, 2002. Expert: Jean-Marie Martin-Hattemberg.
Feder, Soraya. *Divine Beauty: The Art of Collectibles.* Paris: L'Aventurine. 2001.
Fellous, Colette. *Guerlain.* Paris: Denoël, 1987.
Fleck, F. *Flacons à Parfum, Catalogue* for the Perfume Bottle Auction, March 12, 1994; expert: Anne Meter-Seguin.
Fontan, Geneviève. *Cote des Flacons de Parfum Modernes.* Toulouse: Arfon, 1999.
Fontan, Geneviève. *Cote Générale des Cartes Parfumées; Volume III.* Toulouse: Arfon, 1997, 2000.
Fontan, Geneviève. *Cote Générale des Echantillons de Parfum: Nouveautés 98; Nouveautés 99; Nouveautés 2000.* Toulouse: Arfon, 1998, 1999, 2000.
Fontan, Geneviève. *Echantillons Tubes de Parfum.* Toulouse: Arfon, 2000.
Fontan, Geneviève. *Parfums d'Extase.* Toulouse: Arfon, 1996.
Fontan, Geneviève, and Barnouin, Nathalie. *Cote Générale des Echantillons de Parfum.* Toulouse: Editions Fontan & Barnouin, 1996.
Fontan, Geneviève. *Générations Bourjois.* Toulouse: Arfon Maison d'Edition. 2005.
Fontan, Geneviève, and Barnouin, Nathalie. *L'Argus des Echantillons de Parfum.* Toulouse: Editions Milan, 1992.
Fontan, Geneviève, and Barnouin, Nathalie. *La Cote Internationale des Echantillons de Parfum, 1995-1996. Les Echantillons Anciens.* Toulouse: 813 Edition, 1994.
Fontan, Geneviève, and Barnouin, Nathalie. *La Cote Internationale des Echantillons de Parfums Modernes.* Toulouse: 813 Edition, 1995.
Fontan, Geneviève, and Barnouin, Nathalie. *Les Intégrales: Rochas* and *Les Intégrales: Ricci.* Toulouse: Editions Fontan & Barnouin, 1996.
Forsythe, Ruth. *Made in Czechoslovakia.* Marietta, Ohio: Richardson Printing Co., 1982; *Made in Czechoslovakia, Book 2.* Marietta Ohio: Richardson Printing Co., 1993.
Frankl, Beatrice. *Parfum-Flacons.* Augsburg: Battenberg Verlag, 1994.
Gardiner Houlgate. *Perfume Bottles, Sale 6001 [UKPBCC].* October 3, 1998. Expert: Lynda Brine.
Gerson, Roselyn. *Vintage Ladies' Compacts.* Paducah, KY: Collector Books, 1996.
Gerson, Roselyn. *Vintage and Contemporary Purse Accessories.* Paducah, KY: Collector Books, 1997.
Ghozland, F. *Perfume Fantasies.* Toulouse: Editions Milan, 1987.
Green, Annette, and Dyett, Linda. *Secrets of Aromatic Jewelry.* Paris, New York: Flammarion, 1998.
Guinn, Hugh D. *The Glass of René Lalique at Auction.* Tulsa, Oklahoma: Guindex Publications, 1992.
Hymne au Parfum: Catalogue de l'exposition, 1990-1991. Paris: Comité Français du Parfum, 1991.
Johnson, Frances. *Compacts, Powder, and Paint.* Atglen, PA: Schiffer Publishing, 1996.
Jones-North, Jacquelyne. *Czechoslovakian Perfume Bottles and Boudoir Accessories.* Marietta, Ohio: Antique Publications, 1990; revised editon, 1999.
Kaufman, William I. *Perfume.* New York: E. P. Dutton & Co., 1974.
Killian, E. H. *Perfume Bottles Remembered.* Traverse City, Michigan: E. Killian, 1989.
Kozharinov, Veniamin. *Russian Perfumery.* Moscow: Sovetsky Sport, 1998.
La Quinzaine du Parfum. *Perfume Bottle Auction Catalogue* for the sale of October 21, 1994; expert: Creezy Courtoy. Brussels, Belgium.
Latimer, Tirza True. *The Perfume Atomizer: An Object with Atmosphere.* West Chester, Pennsylvania: Schiffer Publishing, 1991.
Leach, Ken. *Perfume Presentation: 100 Years of Artistry.* Toronto: Kres Publishing, 1997.
Lefkowith, Christie Mayer. *The Art of Perfume.* New York: Thames and Hudson, 1994.
Lefkowith, Christie Mayer. *Masterpieces of the Perfume Industry.* New York: Editions Stylissimo, 2000.
Lefkowith, Christie Mayer. *Perfume Presentations Auction.* 8 November, 2003, Geneva Switzerland..
Le Louvre des Antiquaires. *Autour du Parfum du XVIe au XIXe Siècle.* Paris: Le Louvre des Antiquaires, 1985.
Marcilhac, Félix. *R. Lalique: Catalogue Raisonné de l'Oeuvre de Verre.* Paris: Editions de l'Amateur, 1989.
Marsh, Madeleine. *Perfume Bottles: A Collector's Guide.* London: Octopus, Ltd, 1999.
Martin, Hazel. *Figural Perfume and Scent Bottles.* Lancaster, CA: Hazel Martin, 1982.
Martin-Hattemberg, Jean-Marie. *Caron.* Toulouse: Milan Editions, 2000.
Martin-Hattemberg, Jean-Marie. *Le parfum histoire et expertise, Revue Experts, #42, March 1999.*
Martin-Hattemberg, Jean-Marie. *Précieux Effluves / Scentsfully Precious.* Toulouse: Milan Editions, 1997.
Matthews, Leslie G. *The Antiques of Perfume.* London: G. Bell & Sons, 1973.
Mini Flacons. Wiesbaden, Germany: SU Verlag, 1993.
Morris, Edwin T. *Scents of Time: Perfume from Ancient Egypt to the 21st Century.* New York: Metropolitan Museum of Art, 1999.
Mouillefarine, Laurence. *Objets de la Beauté à Collectionner.* Boulogne, France: Éditions MDM, 1999.
Mueller, Laura M. *Collector's Encyclopedia of Compacts: Volumes 1 and 2.* Paducah, KY: Collector Books, 1996.
Neret-Minet. *Flacons à Parfums Catalogue pour les Ventes aux Enchères Publiques,* November 14, 1991; expert: Elisabeth Danenberg.
North, Jacquelyne. *Commercial Perfume Bottles.* West Chester, Pennsylvania: Schiffer Publishing Co, 1987.
North, Jacquelyne. *Perfume, Cologne, and Scent Bottles.* West Chester, Pennsylvania: Schiffer Publishing Co, 1986.
Novy, Petr *Lisovane Sklo a Krystalerie v Jizerskych Horach.* Desna, 2002.
La Parfumerie Française et L'Art dans la Présentation. La Revue des Marques de la Parfumerie et de la Savonnerie: Paris, 1925.
Parfum, Art, et Valeur. Catalogue de Vente, November 15, 1995. Expert: Geneviève Fontan.
Paulson, Paul L. *Guide to Russian Silver Hallmarks.* Paulson: Washington DC, 1976.
Pavia, Fabienne. *The World of Perfume.* New York: Knickerbocker Press, 1995.
Perfume Bottle Quarterly, Volumes 1-15. International Perfume Bottle Association.
Phillips Auctions. *Perfume Presentations.* October 6, 1996, October 26, 1997; October 25, 1998. Geneva, Switzerland. Expert: Christie Mayer Lefkowith. *Perfume Presentations.* November 27, 1999. Zürich, Switzerland; December 10, 2000, New York. Expert: Ken Leach.
René Lalique and Cristal Lalique Perfume Bottles (The Weinstein Collection). New York: Christie's/Lalique Society of America, 1993.
René Lalique et Cie. *Lalique Glass: The Complete Illustrated Catalogue for 1932.* Reprinted by The Corning Museum of Glass, Corning, New York. New York: Dover Publications, 1981.
Restrepo, Federico. *Le Livre d'Heures des Flacons et des Rêves.* Toulouse: Editions Milan, 1995.
Scent Bottles Through the Centuries: the Collection of Joan Hermanowski. St. Petersburg, Florida: Museum of Fine Art, 1997.
Sloan, Jean. *Perfume and Scent Bottle Collecting.* Lombard, Illinois: Wallace-Homestead Co., 1986.
Sotheby's New York. *Important Twentieth Century Decorative Works of Art, including the Mary Lou and Glenn Utt Collection of Lalique.* New York, December 4-5, 1998.
Taylor, Pamela F. *Heavenly Scents.* Privately published, UK, 2000.
Truitt, R. and D. Czech Glass 1918-1939. *Glass Collector's Digest,* Vol. 10, #6, May 1997. pp. 39-46.
Utt, Mary Lou and Glenn. *Lalique Perfume Bottles.* New York: Crown Publishers, 1990. *Updated Addendum Listing and Photo Supplement,* 2001.
Watine-Arnault, D.. *Flacons à Parfums Christian Dior: Catalogue pour la Vente aux Enchères Publiques.* April 12, 1992; expert: Régine de Robien.
Whitmyer, M. & K. *Bedroom and Bathroom Glassware of the Depression Years.* Paducah, Kentucky: Collector Books, 1990.

Important Books Available from Monsen and Baer:

Monsen and Baer publishes these books on American Art Pottery:
The Collectors' Compendium of Roseville Pottery, Volumes I and II.

These books include new historical research and color photos of all the pieces in the pottery lines covered. Price guide information is included in Volume I and a separate price guide accompanies Volume II. Both books are 128 pp each, hardcover, and prices are postpaid.

Volume I - $35

Volume II - $45

These Monsen and Baer Publications are available, all with prices realized: [Shipping: $4.50 for first one, $3.00 for each additional title]:

Monsen and Baer Perfume Bottle Auction I, Chicago, April 6, 1991 @ $18.00. ($25 for International shipment).

Monsen and Baer Perfume Bottle Auction II, Atlanta, May 16, 1992 @ $25.00. ($30 for International shipment).

Monsen and Baer Perfume Bottle Auction III, Dallas, May 1, 1993 @ $28.00. ($35 for International shipment).

Monsen and Baer Perfume Bottle Auction IV, Washington, D. C., May 14, 1994 @ $29.00. ($35 for International shipment).

Monsen and Baer Perfume Bottle Auction V, Chicago, Illinois, May 6, 1995 @ $35.00. ($40 for International shipment).

SOFT COVER

The Beauty of Perfume, *Monsen and Baer Perfume Bottle Auction VI, San Francisco, California, May 11, 1996.* @ $35.00. ($45 for International)

The Legacies of Perfume, *Monsen and Baer Perfume Bottle Auction VII, Washington D. C., May 3, 1997.* @ $45.00 ($65 for International)

Memories of Perfume, *Monsen and Baer Perfume Bottle Auction VIII, Chicago, Illinois., May 16, 1998.* @ $45.00 ($65 for International)

For the Love of Perfume, *Monsen and Baer Perfume Bottle Auction IX, Washington, D. C., May 15, 1999.* @ $45.00 ($65 for International)

A Century of Perfume, *Monsen and Baer Perfume Bottle Auction X, Atlanta, Georgia, May 20, 2000.* @ $45.00 ($65 for International)

The Magic of Perfume, *Monsen and Baer Perfume Bottle Auction XI, Santa Clara, California, May 18, 2001.* @ $45.00 ($65 for International)

The Joy of Collecting Perfume Bottles, *Monsen and Baer Perfume Bottle Auction XII, Dallas, Texas, May 17, 2002.* @ $45.00 ($65 for International)

A Passion for Perfume Bottles, *Monsen and Baer Perfume Bottle Auction XIII, Orlando, Florida, May 16, 2003.* @ $45.00 ($65 for International)

The Wonder of Perfume, *Monsen and Baer Perfume Bottle Auction XIV, Washington D.C., April 30, 2004.* @ $45.00 ($65 for International)

The World of Perfume, *Monsen and Baer Perfume Bottle Auction XV, Dallas, Texas, April 29, 2005.* @ $45.00 ($65 for International)

The Allure of Perfume, *Monsen and Baer Perfume Bottle Auction XVI, Washington, D. C., April 28, 2006.* @ $45.00 ($65 for International)

The Mystique of Perfume, *Monsen and Baer Perfume Bottle Auction XVII, Atlanta, Georgia, May 4, 2007.* @ $45.00 ($65 for International)

HARD COVER

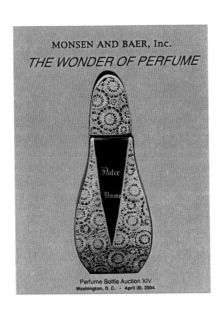

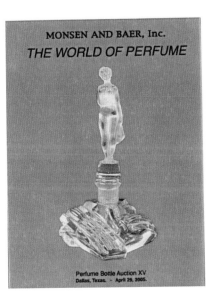

AUCTION LOTS: MINIATURES, SOLIDS, FACTICES

Lot #1. Caron *Farnesiana*, Ciro *New Horizons* and *Reflexions*, Corday *Violette* and *Zigane*, Houbigant *Chantilly*, Hudnut *Yanky Clover* and *Lotus*, Myrurgia *Joya* and *Maja*, in its box, Lucretia Vanterbilt *L. V.*, Worth *Dans la Nuit* and *Je Reviens* [two diff.], Yardley *Lotus, Doux Jasmin*. Sixteen items. Est. $150.00-$250.00.

Lot #2. Chanel *No. 5*, six bottles, all a bit different, *No. 19* and *Cristalle*, Guerlain *Eau Imperiale*, Kerkoff *Djer-Kiss*, Langlois *Caro Nome*, Millot *Crepe de Chine*, Renaud *Orchid*, Ricci *L'Air du Temps*, *Parfum D'Esterel*. Fifteen items. Est. $150.00-$250.00.

Lot #3. Elizabeth Arden *Blue Grass* and *Blue Grass* bath oil; Bourgeois *Evening in Paris* four purse flacons; Lucien Lelong *Balalaika* [2 examples], *Indiscret, Sirocco,* and *Tailspin*; Helena Rubenstein *Apple Blossom Time*. Twelve items. Est. $100.00-$150.00.

Lot #4. Fibah *Chateau Madrid,* Leonid de Lecinskis *No. 9, Orange Blossom Perfume* [four diff. examples], *Blue Waltz* [three diff. examples], *Intermezzo* [three examples]; unidentified candle bottle. Thirteen items. Est. $100.00-$150.00.

Lot #5. Set of eleven miniature perfume bottles and their caps, all less than 2" [5.1 cm]: Givenchy *Le De,* Piguet *Bandit,* Lubin *Nuit de Longchamp,* Ricci *L'Air du Temps* and *Capricci,* Balenciaga *Quadrille,* Lanvin *My Sin,* D'Orsay *Voulez Vous,* Millot *Insolent,* D'Albret *Casaque,* Monteil *Nostalgia,* in their box. Est. $100.00-$200.00.

Lot #6. Les Meilleurs Parfums de Paris boxed set of ten: Balmain *Miss Balmain,* Pucci *Vivara,* Couturier *Coriandre,* Weil *Antilope,* Givenchy *III,* Raphael *Replique,* unidentified one, D'Albret *Ecusson,* Carven *Ma Griffe,* Piguet *Baghari,* in their box. Est. $100.00-$150.00.

Lot #7. Balmain *Vent Vert* [2 diff.], *Jolie Madame* [2 diff.]; Caron *Bellodgia* [2 examples]; Coty *Emeraude* and *L'Aimant;* Dana *Tabu* [2 diff.]; D'Orsay *Intoxication,* Le *Dandy, Voulez Vous;* Fragonard *Zizanie;* Givenchy *L'Interdit;* Griffe *Grilou;* Lancôme *Magie;* Lenthéric *Miracle* and *Red Lilac;* Lubin *Nuit de Longchamps* [2 diff.]; Marquay *Prince Douka* and *Coup de Feu;* Matchabelli *Summer Frost;* Millot *Crêpe de Chine* [2 examples]; Patou *1000;* Shulton *Desert Flower;* Vigny *Heure Intime; Irresistible.* Thirty items. Est. $200.00-$300.00.

9

Lot #8. Coty lot of eight miniature bottles including *L'Aimant* [two diff.], *Emeraude* [three diff.], *Paris, Asuma,* and *Muguet des Bois,* smallest 1.4" [3.6 cm], some with perfume. Eight items. Est. $100.00-$200.00.

Lot #9. Lucien Lelong *Tailspin, Sirôcco, Taglio, Balalaika, Opening Night, Orgueil, Tempest, Indiscret* tester set of eight fragrances, each approximately 2" tall [5.1 cm], with their labels. Est. $400.00-$600.00.

Lot #10. Dana *Emir, Bolero,* and *Tabu* clear glass miniature bottles with black caps, 2" [5.1 cm], labels on front, bottom of each bottle signed *Dana,* in their box and outer box marked #133. Est. $100.00-$200.00.

Lot #11. Le Galion *Lily of the Valley* clear glass bottle and stopper, 1.9" [4.8 cm], full and sealed, in its box. Est. $100.00-$150.00.

Lot #12. Ciro *Acclaim, Danger, New Horizons, Reflexions, Surrender* clear glass bottles with red caps shaped as flowers, 1.7" [4.3 cm], with advertising flyer, in its box. Est. $75.00-$125.00.

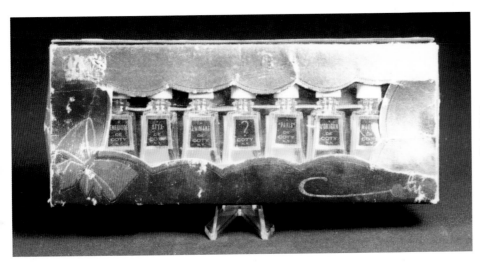

Lot #13. Coty *Perfume Prize Package* set of seven fragrances: *Emeraude, Styx, L'Aimant, ?, Paris, L'Origan,* and *Muguet,* each 1.6" [4.1 cm], in their green Christmas case. Est. $75.00-$150.00.

Lot #14. Fabergé *Woodhue* miniature glass bottle and wooden cap, 2.4" [6.1 cm], in its tiny pouch and box, some perfume. Est. $50.00-$75.00.

Lot #15. Lucien Lelong *Indiscret* and *Sirocco* clear glass miniatures with gold caps, 2" [5.1 cm], the back with the Lelong logo, one with box. Est. $100.00-$150.00.

Lot #16. Niki de Saint Phalle blue glass bottles with gold caps, 1.8", 2.1", 2.9" [4.5 cm, 5.3 cm, 7.4 cm], all with a decoration of colorful painted snakes. Three items. Est. $150.00-$250.00.

Lot #17. Lucien Lelong *Tailspin, Carefree, Indiscret, Inpromptu,* clear glass bottles with turret shaped white plastic stoppers, 2.8" [7.1 cm], empty, in their white plastic holder. Est. $100.00-$200.00.

Lot #18. Guerlain *Mitsouko* clear glass minature bottle and stopper, 2.3" [5.8 cm], empty, label on front; Corday *Muguet* two clear glass miniature bottles, 1.7" and 2" [4.3 cm and 5.1 cm], empty, labels around neck. Three items. Est. $100.00-$200.00.

Lot #19. Le Galion set of six miniature bottles and their brass screw on caps: *Jasmin, Sortilège, Lily of the Valley, Gardénia, Bourrasque, Brumes,* 2.1" [5.3 cm], in their red box. Est. $100.00-$200.00.

Lot #20. Coty *Le Vertige* clear glass bottle and gold cap, 2.2" [5.6 cm], gold label at center, in its pretty little box. Est. $100.00-$150.00.

Lot #21. Richard Hudnut *Tenfold Lily of the Valley* clear glass bottle and frosted glass stopper, 3.4" [8.6 cm], gold label at center, some perfume and sealed, in its gray box. Est. $100.00-$200.00.

Lot #22. Dana *Tabu* clear glass miniature bottle in the shape of a violin with black cap, 2.5" [6.4 cm], full of perfume, in its box marked "not for sale." Est. $100.00-$150.00.

Lot #23. Lucien Lelong *Joli Bouquet Orage, Indiscret, Passionnement* clear glass bottles with brass caps, 2" [5.1 cm], gold labels on front, in their box. Est. $50.00-$150.00.

Lot #24. Lucien Lelong *Tout Lelong Mélodie* and *Mon Image* three clear glass bottles with silver metal caps, 2" [5.1 cm], silver labels on front, in their box. Est. $50.00-$150.00.

Lot #25. Houbigant *Quelques Fleurs* clear glass bottle and stopper, 3.6" [9.1 cm], decorated with a tassel on the side, gold label underneath, in its original box. Est. $50.00-$100.00.

Lot #26. Coty *L'Origan, L'Effleurt, Violette Pourpre* three clear glass bottles with glass stoppers and long daubers, tallest, 2.2" [5.6 cm], [one with cracked neck], bottom of each signed *Coty.* Est. $100.00-$200.00.

Lot #27. Elizabeth Arden *Mémoire Chérie* clear glass bottle and stopper, 2.5" [6.4 cm], sealed with perfume, in its lavender box. Est. $150.00-$250.00.

Lot #28. Le Galion *Bourrasque, Gardénia, Sortilège, Tubéreuse,* 1.8" [4.5 cm], labels on front and on top of bottles, in their box. Est. $100.00-$200.00.

Lot #29. Lenthéric *Cabaña* clear glass bottle and stopper, 2.2" [5.6 cm], label on front, in its box. Est. $75.00-$125.00.

Lot #30. Caron *Nuit de Noel* ['Night of Christmas'] clear glass bottle with gold cap, 2" [5.1 cm], gold label on bottle, funnel, and gold *flacon de sac,* all in their box. Est. $100.00-$200.00.

Lot #31. Lucien Lelong *Indiscret* two clear glass bottles with white caps, 1.5" and 3.2" [3.8 and 8.1 cm], labels on the front of each bottle, in their pretty red box. Est. $150.00-$250.00.

Lot #32. Guerlain *L'Heure Bleue* clear glass bottle and stopper, 2.8" [7.1 cm], in its beautiful box and outer box. Est. $100.00-$150.00.

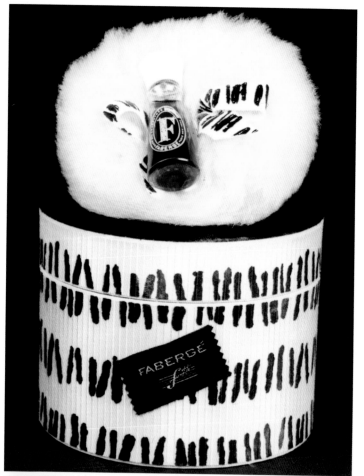

Lot #33. Max Factor *Epris* glass bottle and silver cap, 1.7" [4.3 cm], held by a tiny doll, label on bottom. Est. $75.00-$125.00.

Lot #34. Herbert Roystone *Poudre L'Amé* face powder and dusting powder, with advertising booklet; Roger and Gallet *Pavots d'Argent* body powder and puff, unopened; Fabergé *F#* miniature perfume bottle and puff and bath powder, in their box. Three items. Est. $100.00-$200.00.

Lot #35. Bourjois *Evening in Paris* talcum blue bottle with metal cap; Bourjois unidentified clear bottle; Richard Hudnut *Yanky Clover* with pink cap, in its box; D'Orsay *Intoxication*, in its box; Coty *Le Vertige;* Pascal Morabito *Or Noir;* Lucretia Vanderbilt powder, rouge, and lipstick. Seven items. Est. $200.00-$300.00.

Lot #36. Lenthéric *Tweed* [originally Risque-Tout in French] clear glass bottle, inner glass stopper and wood overcap, 2.2" [5.5 cm], name in black enamel, in a book presentation called *A Christmas Carol* whose frontespiece is a song: "Jingle Bells, Jingle Bells, Jingle all the Way, Oh What Fun it is to give a Lenthéric gift this day!" Est. $150.00-$250.00.

Lot #37. Coty *Paris* clear glass bottle and blue cap, 3.5" [8.9 cm], label on front and bottom marked *Coty*, with unopened *Air Spun* powder, in a Christmas novelty display. Est. $75.00-$150.00.

Lot #38. Elizabeth Arden *Blue Grass* dusting powder and *Stop Red* lipstick, in a candy cane presentation for Christmas. Est. $150.00-$250.00.

Lot #39. Prince Matchabelli *Ave Maria, Duchess of York, Katherine the Great* clear glass crown bottles with gold tops, 1.3" [3.3 cm], in their brass bell marked *Prince Matchabelli*, with Merry Christmas sticker. Est. $200.00-$300.00.

Lot #40. Lucien Lelong *Perfume B* glass bottle and stopper, 2.2" [5.6 cm], with label and unopened; *Taglio* glass bottle and stopper, 2.6" [6.6 cm]; *Indiscret* glass bottle and stopper, 3" [7.6 cm], in its box; two Lelong bottles, one empty, 2.1" and 2.5" [5.3 and 6.4 cm]. Five items. Est. $200.00-$300.00.

Lot #42. Elizabeth Arden *Blue Grass* clear glass bottle and gold top, 2.7" [6.8 cm], perfume atomizer, and flower mist, all full, in their box. Est. $300.00-$400.00.

Lot #43. Coty *Emeraude, L'Origan, L'Aimant* set of three clear glass bottles and frosted glass stoppers, 1.7" [4.3 cm], the bottoms all stamped *Coty,* in their smart red presentation box. Est. $200.00-$300.00.

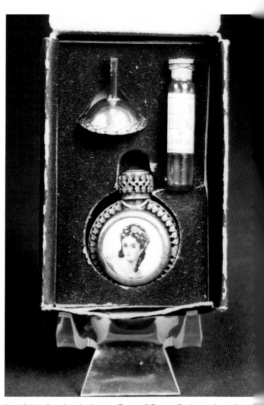

Lot #41. Lucien Lelong *Orage* ['Storm'] clear glass bottle with tiny rubber stopper, 1.5" [3.8 cm], in a box with met funnel and tiny bottle with a woman, in their box. Es $200.00-$300.00.

Lot #44. Matchabelli *Windsong* clear glass bottle and gold metal cap, 1.7" [4.3 cm], enameled green and gold, bottom with label, in its black box. Est. $150.00-$250.00.

Lot #45. Elizabeth Arden *For Her* rare miniature perfume, 2.4" [6.1 cm], in its dark green and gold purse with unused lipstick, powder, comb and mirror, in its box. Est. $500.00-$750.00.

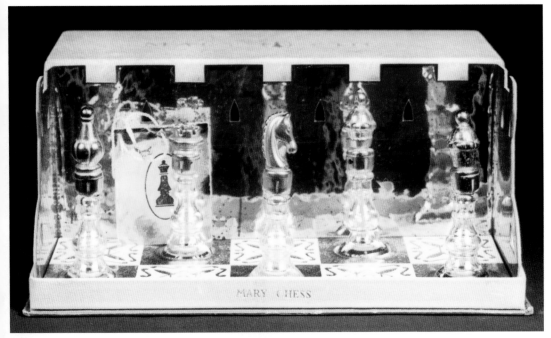

Lot #46. Mary Chess set of five: *Tapestry* [the Knight], *White Lilac* [the Castle], *Song* [the King], *Yram* [the Queen], *Strategy* [the Bishop] clear glass bottles with gold metal tops, tallest 3" [15 cm] with tiny pamphlet, in their box. Est. $600.00-$800.00.

Lot #47. Lucien Lelong *Indiscret* clear glass bottle and gold screw on stopper, 1.7" [4.3 cm], label on front and bottom of bottle, in its box. Est. $100.00-$150.00.

Lot #48. Dana *20 Carats, Tabu, Ambush* each 1.6" [4 cm] clear glass bottles and gold caps, all in their box. Est. $150.00-$200.00.

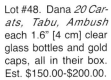

Lot #49. Prince Matchabelli *Princess Norina, Ave Maria, Duchess of York* clear glass bottle and brass metal caps, 1.6" [4 cm], labels front and back, in their tiny green box. Est. $150.00-$250.00.

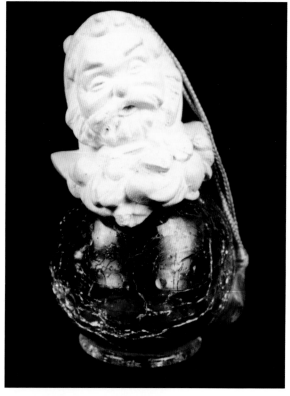

Lot #50. Lucien Lelong *Whisper* clear crackle glass bottle with a plaster Santa's head stopper, 3.5" [8.9 cm]; this was meant to be hung as a Christmas ornament. Est. $150.00-$250.00.

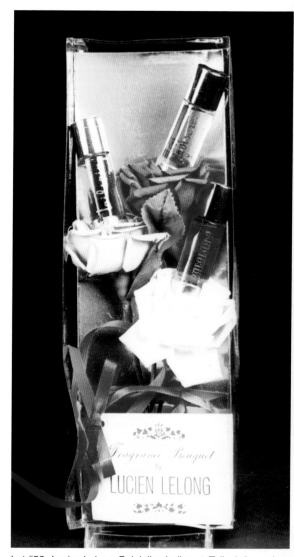

Lot #52. Lucien Lelong *Balalaika, Indiscret, Tailspin* three clear glass bottles with gold caps, each 2.4" [6.1 cm], each mounted in the center of a red, white, and pink rose, in their box. Est. $200.00-$300.00.

Lot #51. Lenthéric *Pink Party* clear glass bottle and gold cap, 2.3" [5.8 cm], yellow label at the center, in its pretty yellow box. Est. $100.00-$150.00.

Lot #53. Elizabeth Arden *Blue Grass* clear glass bottle and turquoise cap, 1.8" [4.6 cm], silver and turquoise label on front. This is a seldom seen replica miniature. Est. $200.00-$300.00.

#54. Schiaparelli *Shocking de Schiaparelli* set of four miniature replica bottles with gold caps, each 1.4" [3.6 cm], some perfume in each [unused condition], round gold S label at center of each, in a Roulette Wheel box with the numbers 1 to 4; the bottles form the separation of these numbers on the wheel, and a white heart denotes the winning number; the pink and gold box is decorated with these numbers. When a button is pushed to open the box, spring mechanism makes the wheel revolve. This is a rare and wonderful Schiaparelli presentation in very fresh condition. Est. $1,500.00-$2,500.00.

#55. Ciro *Danger* clear glass bottle and gold screw-on cap, 2.2" [5.6 , in its small black pouch and box. Est. $150.00-$250.00.

Lot #56. Caron *With Pleasure* clear glass bottle and stopper, 2.2" [5.5 cm], in a barrel shape, full of perfume, labels at neck and on bottom, names in gold on front, in its mint condition box and outer box. Est. $400.00-$600.00.

Lot #57. Coty *Emeraude* clear glass bottle with green plastic cap, 2.2" [5.5 cm], with *Air Spun* powder in unopened box, all in their original box. Est. $250.00-$350.00.

Lot #58. Richard Hudnut *Three Flowers* set: lipstick [used], powder compact, and clear glass bottle and frosted stopper with long dauber, gold label, in their box. Est. $200.00-$300.00.

Lot #59. Matchabelli *Golden Jubilee Stradivari* clear glass bottles and their white caps, 2.4" and 1.4" [6 and 3.5 cm], full of perfume, gold labels on bottom, in their box. Est. $100.00-$200.00.

Lot #60. Elizabeth Arden *Perfume Pins,* each of two, mounted in a pretty box with flowers, also with outer box. Est. $250.00-$350.00.

Lot #61. Corday *Jet, L'Ardente Nuit, Zigane,* 1.3" [3.3 cm], held in an elaborate ashtray, 8" [20.3 cm], which is fashioned like a lampost on the Rue de la Paix, the bottom impressed *Corday.* Est. $375.00-$475.00.

Lot #62. Coty *Paris* frosted glass perfume vial, 2.5" [6.4 cm], *Geranium* lipstick [unused], and powder compact with *Soleil d'Or* powder in their beautiful blue velvet case. Est. $400.00-$600.00.

Lot #63. Lucien Lelong *Sirôcco* clear glass bottle and stopper, 2.9" [7.4 cm], label near base and on the bottom, in its pink and gold armoire box. Est. $100.00-$200.00.

Lot #64. Elizabeth Arden *Blue Grass* miniature bottle and glass stopper, 2" [5.1 cm], showing a blue glass horse inside, some perfume, in its box, in a box from Gladdings in Providence, Rhode Island. Est. $1,250.00-$1,750.00.

Lot #65. Lucien Lelong *Mon Image* clear glass bottle and stopper, 1.6" [4.1 cm], label on front and back, in its mirrored box with Lelong label. Est. $200.00-$300.00.

Lot #66. Lucien Lelong *Murmure* ['Whisper'] clear glass bottle and stopper, 1.9" [4.8 cm], label on the front, in its box bottom. Est. $300.00-$400.00.

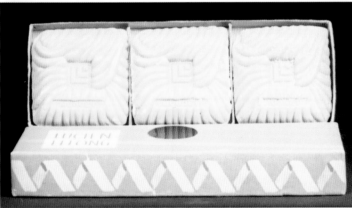

Lot #67. Lucien Lelong *Muguet* ['Lily of the Valley'] and *Sirôcco* boxed soaps, in their box, unused. Est. $50.00-$75.00.

Lot #68. Vigny *Le Golliwogg* clear glass bottle and red plastic cap, 2" [5.1 cm], the label on the front is marked *pour le mouchoir* 'for the handkerchief,' in its box. Est. $100.00-$200.00.

Lot #69. Molinard *Concreta Carino* [orange], *Fleurettes* [blue], *Naniko* [green], *Tabatchin* [red], *Xmas Bells* [white] set of five bakelite dice, .8" [2 cm], in their brown leather case. Est. $400.00-$600.00.

Lot #70. Mary Chess *Tapestry* gold solid, 1.4" x 1.8" [3.6 x 4.5 cm], a fleur de lys in gemstones at center, with its label and perfume, back marked with a chesspiece, in its box. Est. $150.00-$250.00.

Lot #71. Estée Lauder *pleasures* solid perfume of a dog in a bath bucket with soap bubbles, 1.1" [2.8 cm], stamped *Estée Lauder 2002*. Est. $75.00-$125.00.

Lot #72. Max Factor solid perfume fawn, 1.2" [3 cm], with perfume, signed inside, on a long gold chain; unsigned elephant, 1.1" [2.8 cm], with perfume, and also on a long chain. Est. $75.00-$125.00.

Lot #73. Lionceau *Poème Arabe* pair of red bakelite dice for solid perfume, 1" [2.5 cm] each one signed *Lionceau Place de L'Opera,* in their tiny box. Est. $400.00-$600.00.

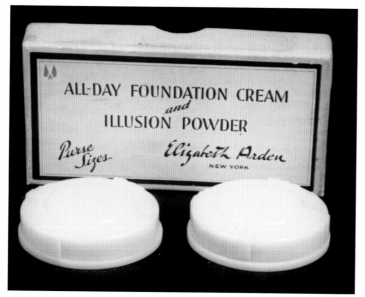

Lot #74. Elizabeth Arden *All-Day Foundation Creme* and *Illusion Powder,* two unused compacts, in their box. Est. $75.00-$150.00.

Lot #75. Lucien Lelong *Impromptu* dusting powder in its large box, 3.2" [8.1 cm], with the starburst motif. Est. $75.00-$150.00.

Lot #76. Elizabeth Arden face powder in a compact with a design of red and white circles on the top, puff marked *Arden,* in its box. Est. $150.00-$250.00.

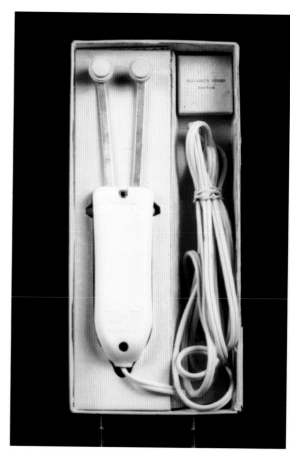

Lot #77. Elizabeth Arden velvet touch face vibrator, in working condition, with box bottom and a small box with additional tips. Est. $75.00-$150.00.

Lot #78. Elizabeth Arden *Blue Grass Sachets* set of five sachets in blue and gold, in their box. Est. $100.00-$150.00.

Lot #79. Houbigant *Toujours Moi* perfume solid of two lovebirds on a perch in a cage, 2.5" [6.4 cm], with perfume, label on bottom. Est. $75.00-$125.00.

Lot #80. Lucien Lelong *Bright Red* green jeweled lipstick, 2.2" [5.5 cm], signed with Lucien Lelong logo on top. Est. $100.00-$150.00.

Lot #81. Ultima *Ciara* solid perfume compact, 1.8" [4.5 cm], the front with a lady's portrait under glass, label on the back, with perfume. Est. $75.00-$125.00.

Lot #82. Elizabeth Arden compact, 2.2" [5.5 cm], topped with red stones, unused condition, in its original box. Est. $300.00-$400.00.

Lot #83. Caron *Nocturnes* gold metal jewelry that is meant as a holder for perfume, about 1" [2.5 cm] in size, on its black cord and pouch and box. Est. $100.00-$200.00.

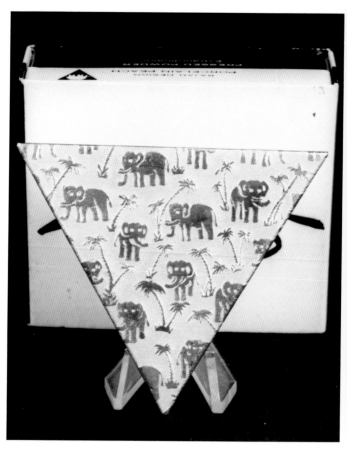

Lot #84. Perfume solid in the shape of a Teddy Bear, 2.6" [6.6 cm], empty, with loop and gold necklace, in its box, unmarked but probably Max Factor. Est. $75.00-$125.00.

Lot #85. Fabergé *Porcelain Peach* powder in a triangular powder compact, with powder refill and tiny advertising compact, in its box. Est. $100.00-$150.00.

Lot #86. Mary Chess *Tapestry* perfume solid heart, 1.6" long [4 cm], decorated with a couple on the front and flowers on the back, some perfume present, with its label, in its box. Est. $150.00-$250.00.

Lot #87. Elizabeth Arden *Crème Extraordinaire* ceramic pot and cover, 4.4" [11.2 cm], empty, in its box. Est. $200.00-$300.00.

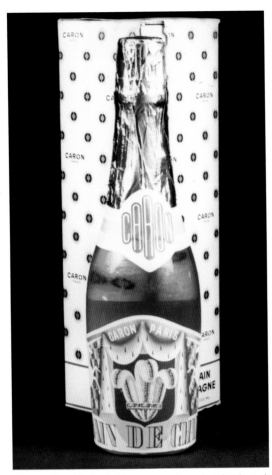

Lot #88. Caron *Royal Bain de Champagne* clear glass bottle and stopper, 10.5" [26.7 cm], made to look like a wine bottle, full and sealed, in its box. Est. $200.00-$300.00.

Lot #89. Lucien Lelong *Indiscret* huge frosted glass bottle, 12" [30.4 cm], near full and sealed; this is the reintroduced bottle of the perfume. Est. $500.00-$750.00.

PERFUME LAMPS, CROWN TOP BOTTLES

Lot #90. Coty early clear and frosted glass powder dish, with brown stain, 2" [5.1 cm], showing two women embracing, bottom signed *Coty*. Est. $350.00-$450.00.

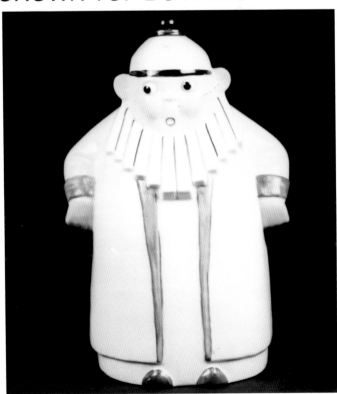

Lot #91. Adorable boudoir light in the shape of a Mandarin, 9.5" [24 cm], looking very excited, painted in many colors, unwired, faintly marked *Germany* and with illegible mold numbers. Est. $300.00-$500.00.

Lot #92. Perfume lamp in the shape of two cats, 6.9" [17.5 cm], both looking to the side, one in black and white and the other in brown and white, unwired, of German manufacture. Est. $175.00-$275.00.

Lot #93. Perfume lamp in the shape of a cat, 6.5" [16.5 cm], sitting pertly on a tasseled pillow, painted in brown and white, of German manufacture, model #12077, unwired. Est. $150.00-$250.00.

Lot #94. Crown top bottle shaped as a duck, 3.4" [8.7 cm], in yellow, orange and black, entirely unmarked, made in Germany. Est. $125.00-$200.00.

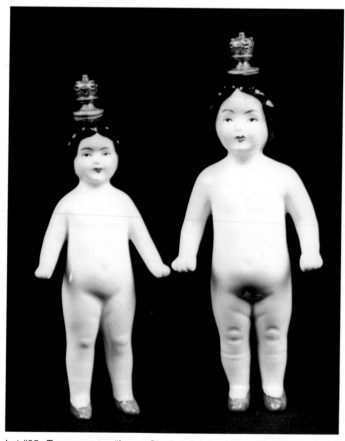

Lot #95. Two crown top "frozen Charlotte" dolls, 5.5" and 6.5" [14 and 16.5 cm], probably for perfume or bath oils, the back impressed *Germany 3151 and 3150*. Est. $200.00-$300.00.

Lot #96. Crown top bottle shaped as a woman in a cloche hat, 2.2" [5.5 cm], marked *Germany* and with mold numbers *8056*. Est. $200.00-$300.00.

Lot #97. Crown top bottle shaped as stylized womans head with a long earring, 2.3" [5.8 cm], marked *Germany* and with mold numbers *8055*. Est. $200.00-$300.00.

Lot #98. Crown top bottle shaped as woman with a pink cloche hat, 2.2" [5.5 cm] marked *Germany* and with mold numbers *8051*. Est. $200.00-$300.00.

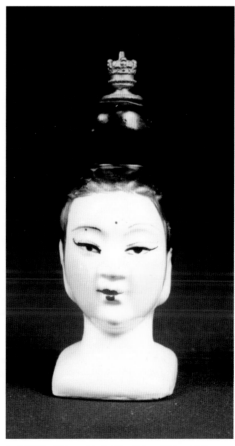

Lot #99. Crown top bottle in the form of a smiling puppy, 2.7" [6.9 cm], the bottom with an Irice label, and stamped *Germany*. Est. $125.00-$175.00.

Lot #100. Crown top bottle shaped as a pirate with a blue hat, 2.3" [5.8 cm] marked *Germany* and with mold numbers *8057*. Est. $250.00-$350.00.

Lot #101. Crown top bottle shaped as an oriental woman's head, 3.5" [8.9 cm], completely unmarked, probably of German manufacture. Est. $300.00-$400.00.

Lot #102. Pair of decorative bottles, 7.6" [19.3 cm], each bottle four sided and decorated with five circles, bottoms unmarked. Est. $100.00-$150.00.

Lot #103. Green, white, and gold slag glass bottle, 4.5" [11.4 cm], with two applied handles on the sides of the perfectly round bottle, with its inner stopper and green jewel on the stopper, probably of Bohemian or Czechoslovakian manufacture. Est. $200.00-$300.00.

Lot #104. Black glass bottle and clear glass stopper, 5.6" [14.2 cm], in the Czechoslovakian style, unmarked. Est. $100.00-$150.00.

Lot #105. Green glass bottle and stopper, 3.4" [8.6 cm], the bottle overlaid in silver, the center medallion with the initial J, unmarked. Est. $200.00-$300.00.

Lot #106. Blue glass perfume bottle, inner stopper, and silver cap, 1.6" [4.1 cm], bearing the British hallmarks for Birmingham, 1916. Est. $100.00-$200.00.

Lot #107. Small powder jar in the shape of a lady in green dress, inscribed *7743;* two small pin dishes in the shape of bathing beauties marked *4030* and *4090*, one marked Germany in the mold. Est. $100.00-$150.00.

Lot #108. Pair of bottles with glass stoppers, 3" [7.6 cm], metal collars around the neck, held in a metal holder that is highly jeweled, bottom marked *Austria*. Est. $300.00-$500.00.

Lot #109. Dresser set of one large bowl, 4.2" [10.7 cm] and two small ones, 1.6" [4 cm], with silver caps, all marked *Sterling*. Three items. Est. $125.00-$175.00.

Lot #110. Pretty green glass atomizer, 6.2" [15.7 cm], decorated with a pretty design in gold and a peach color, new ball and tassel, bottom unsigned, but probably of European manufacture. Est. $100.00-$200.00.

Lot #111. Clear crystal bottle and atomizer pump, 3" [7.6 cm], cut with a flower on both sides, white enamel on the atomizer, side of atomizer marked *sterling silver* and with maker's mark, unmarked. Est. $150.00-$250.00.

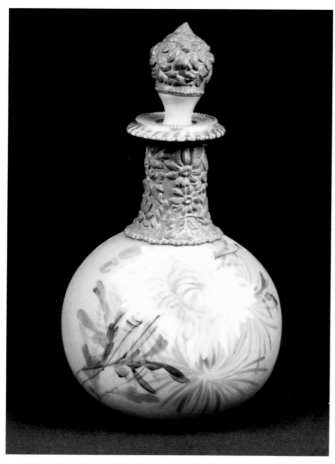

Lot #112. Beautiful Mt. Washington type bottle with glass stopper, 7.5"
[19 cm], painted with crysanthemums, with Pairpoint metal stopper, circa
1895, unsigned. Est. $600.00-$750.00.

Lot #113. Clear glass bottle with glass inner stopper and silver cap, 4.2"
[10.7 cm], the bottle with a red design showing a woman and a bird,
unsigned. Est. $400.00-$600.00.

Lot #114. Dark green glass bottle and stopper covered with a silver
overlay with *Duluth* spelled out, 3.5" [8.9 cm], unmarked bottom. Est.
$100.00-$200.00.

Lot #115. Early twentieth century porcelain bottle and stopper, 9" [22.9
cm], painted with a bird and various motifs, some wear to the gold around
the neck, of continental manufacture. Est. $250.00-$350.00.

Lot #116. French red enamelled perfume bottle, inner stopper,and overcap, 3" [7.6 cm], a beautiful design of red, white, and gold in perfect condition, with silver mountings, unsigned. Est. $1,000.00-$1,200.00.

Lot #117. Beautiful turquoise blue bottle and silver cap, 3.9" [9.9 cm], unsigned. Est. $300.00-$400.00.

Lot #118. Beautiful set of four bottles of clear crystal with small stoppers and long daubers, 3.7" [9.4 cm], set with green, red and amber jewels, probably of Czechoslovakian manufacture. Est. $750.00-$1,000.00.

Lot #119. Superb set of four bottles of black crystal with clear and green tops, 5" [12.7 cm], the elaborate case of gold metal set with green stones and pearls, gold collars, each stopper with its long dauber, bottom of the case is marked *Austria*. Est. $2,500.00-$3,500.00.

Lot #120. Clear over white glass perfume bottle and stopper, 9.3" [14 cm], both stopper and bottle mounted with medallions of green glass, with traces of gold enamel, possibly of Bohemian manufacture. Est. $250.00-$450.00.

Lot #121. Beautiful quality green glass bottle and stopper, 9.7" [24.6 cm], the extremely long neck molded with a snake, enameled in gold, possibly of French manufacture. Est. $500.00-$750.00.

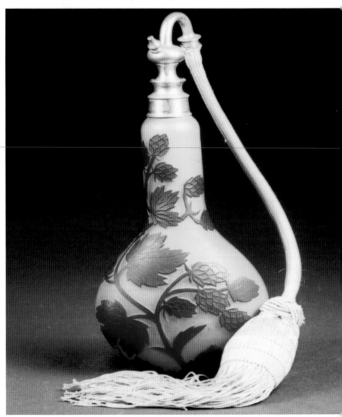

Lot #122. Very elegant baluster form cobalt blue bottle with matching stopper and long dauber, 6.7" [17 cm], the bottle decorated in gold with an elaborate design, neck signed *Czechoslovakia*. Est. $250.00-$350.00.

Lot #123. Richard art glass atomizer bottle of orange glass overlaid with dark red, 8.7" [22.1 cm], cut with a flower motif, bottom signed *Richard*. Est. $800.00-$1,200.00.

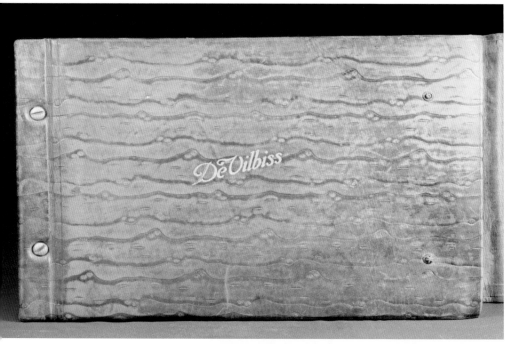

Lot #124. The DeVilbiss catalogue dated 1927. Est. $5,000.00-$7,500.00.

Lot #125. The DeVilbiss catalogue for 1928. Est. $5,000.00-$7,500.00.

Lot #126. DeVilbiss powder jar, 3" [7.6 cm], entirely enameled in gold and with handpainted flowers on the lid, unsigned. Est. $100.00-$150.00.

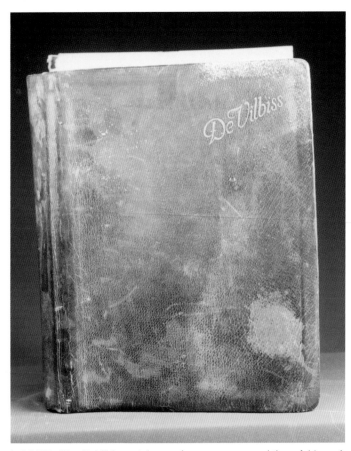

Lot #127. The DeVilbiss catalogues for many years and three folders of original blueprints for many DeVilbiss items. Est. $1,000.00-$2,000.00.

Lot #128. Frosted glass atomizer bottle with a brass cap and tassel, 5" [12.7 cm], the bottle molded with flowers, the bottom signed *DeVilbiss*. Est. $150.00-$250.00.

Lot #129. Coty *Emeraude* milk glass bottle and atomizer top, 5" [12.7 cm], with green enamel painting of a garden all around the bottle, label on bottom. Est. $50.00-$100.00.

Lot #130. Porcelain bottle with atomizer attachment, 5.5" [14 cm], molded as a black boy holding an urn, painted in multicolors, the bottom molded *3108* and with a crossed swords mark. Est. $200.00-$300.00.

Lot #131. DeVilbiss Imperial glass matched set of bottles, the tallest is 7.8" [20 cm], with violet and yellow jewels all around, the atomizer bottle signed *DeVilbiss* on the bottom. Est. $17,500.00-$22,500.00.

Lot #132. Orange bottle and stopper, 7" [17.8 cm], enameled in gold and internally decorated in orange, signed *DeVilbiss*. Est. $400.00-$600.00.

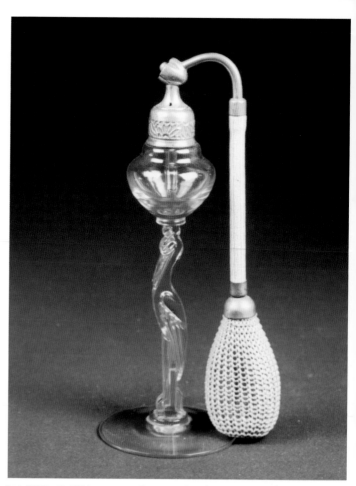

Lot #133. DeVilbiss green glass atomizer in the shape of bird, 6.4" [16.2 cm], original ball and tassel, apparently unsigned. Est. $1,200.00-$1,500.00.

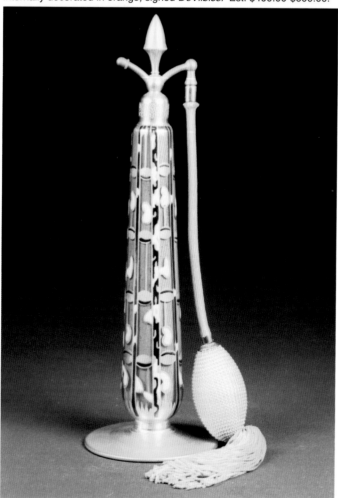

Lot #134. DeVilbiss perfume atomizer, 10.2" [25.9 cm], the exterior decorated in green, gold, and black, the interior in purple, new ball and tassel, bottom faintly signed *DeVilbiss*. Est. $1,500.00-$2,000.00.

Lot #135. Spectacular light pink and white Imperial glass bottle and its atomizer top, 7" [17.8 cm], original atomizer ball [hardened], bottom signed *DeVilbiss*. Est. $6,000.00-$8,000.00.

Lot #136. Guerlain *L'Heure Bleue* ['Twilight'] clear crystal bottle and stopper of inverted heart shape, 4.7" [12 cm], round label on front, signed *Baccarat* at center, Bacc. ref. #171 [1947]; Guerlain *Shalimar* clear crystal bottle, 4.5" [11.4 cm], gold label on front, signed *Baccarat* at center. Bacc #597 [1926]. Two items. Est. $100.00-$150.00.

Lot #137. Guerlain *Mitsouko* clear crystal bottle and stopper of inverted heart shape, 4" [10.2 cm], empty, round label on front, signed *Baccarat* at center, Bacc. ref. #171 [1947]. Est. $100.00-$150.00.

Lot #138. Houbigant *Chantilly* clear crystal bottle and stopper, 7.6" [19.3 cm], with a gold picture of 17th century life at the bottom, signed with Baccarat emblem on bottom, in its red box. Est. $500.00-$750.00.

Lot #139. Christian Dior *Diorling* clear crystal bottle and stopper, 6.5" [16.5 cm], shaped as an amphora with rings molded on either side, empty, name in white enamel, signed *Baccarat* in emblem on the bottom, in its beautiful yellow box. Bacc. #820 [1957]. Est. $400.00-$600.00.

Lot #140. D'Orsay *Toujours Fidèle* ['Ever Faithful'] clear crystal bottle in pillow form with stopper topped by a sitting dog with brown patina, 3.3" [8.5 cm], names enameled in black, in its sumptuous gold-lined box of pyramid shape, signed *Crystal Nancy*. Est. $1,000.00-$1,500.00.

Lot #141. Corday *Orchidée Bleue* extremely large size [probably factice], 5" [12.7 cm], a flowerform motif, label lacking, empty, signed *Baccarat* in emblem. Est. $250.00-$350.00.

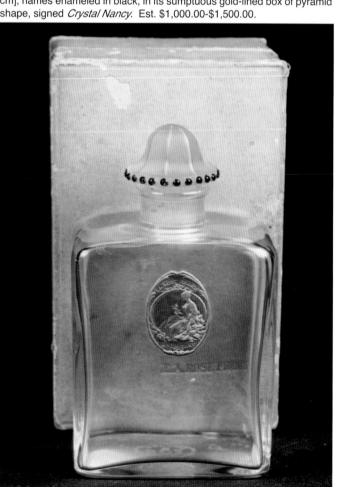

Lot #142. Houbigant *La Rose France* clear crystal bottle and stopper, 4.2" [10.7 cm]; gold label on front of bottle showing a woman with flowers, bottom signed *Baccarat,* in its box. Bacc. #443 [1920]. Est. $500.00-$750.00.

Lot #143. Jean Patou *Amour Amour* clear crystal bottle and stopper, 3.5" [8.9 cm], empty, gold and blue labels on front, bottom signed *Jean Patou* in acid, in its cream and gold box. Bacc. #531 [1924]. Est. $500.00-$750.00.

Coty *L'Or* ['Gold'] clear crystal bottle and stopper, 6.2" [15.7 cm], of teardrop form, full of perfume, signed *Baccarat* on the bottom, in its beautiful light yellow box. Bacc. #821 [1959]. Est. $1,500.00-$2,000.00.

Lot #145. Wolff Frères *Crisance* very fine clear crystal bottle and stopper, 5" [12.7 cm], of ball shape with dauber internally decorated with intertwined swirls, unopened condition, bottom signed *Steuben,* in its elegant gray suede case lined with silk and blue velvet. Circa 1948. Est. $2,500.00-$3,500.00.

Lot #146. Ybry *Femme de Paris* huge size green over white crystal bottle and inner stopper with green enameled overcap, empty, in a beautiful green leather box with a heart shaped medallion showing a cupid and a butterfly. Est. $1,500.00-$2,500.00.

Lot #147. Ybry *Joie de Vivre* ['The Joy of Living'] clear crystal bottle and stopper, 3" [7.6 cm], gold label at the center, full and sealed, unsigned, in its cream colored box. Bacc. #583 [1925-1927]. Est. $800.00-$1,200.00.

Lot #148. Guerlain *Shalimar* clear crystal bottle and blue stopper, 3.9" [10 cm], gold label, signed *Baccarat* on bottom as well as the original price tag from Bullocks Los Angeles, in its box. Est. $100.00-$200.00.

Lot #149. Caron unidentified perfume, 6.2" [15.7 cm], the bottle with gold doré lions on the sides of the bottle, signed *Baccarat,* in its beautiful black box. Bacc. #812 [1948]. Est. $1,500.00-$2,000.00.

Lot #150. Houbigant *La Rose France* clear crystal bottle and stopper, 4" [10.2 cm], impressed with a gorgeous label showing a courtier smelling flowers, unsigned, in its box. Bacc. #29 [1908]. Est. $400.00-$600.00.

Lot #151. Rimmel *Vocalise* clear crystal bottle, inner stopper, and overcap, 3.2" [8 cm], with its perfume, names in gold enamel, in its red box, signed *Baccarat* on base. Bacc. #522 [1923]. Est. $1,000.00-$1,500.00.

Lot #152. Ciro *Danger* unusual clear crystal bottle, inner stopper, and massive black crystal overcap, 4.1" [10.5 cm], some perfume, names in gold enamel on overcap, bottom signed *Baccarat* in emblem, in its smart red and black box. Bacc. #777 [1938]. Est. $400.00-$600.00.

Lot #153. Coty *L'Origan* clear crystal bottle and inner stopper with brass overcap, label on front, empty, cap is signed *Coty Paris*, bottom signed *Baccarat*. Bacc. #227 [1913]. This is a very early bottle. Est. $300.00-$400.00.

Lot #154. Guerlain *Coque d'Or* ['Bow of Gold'], 3" [7.6 cm], in the form of a bowtie, Baccarat emblem on the bottom. Bacc. #770 [1937]. Est. $400.00-$500.00.

Lot #155. Houbigant *Le Parfum d'Argeville* clear crystal bottle and stopper, 4.1" [10.4 cm], the bottle decorated with a beautiful pastoral with a shepherdess and her sheep, with perfume, names in gold, bottom signed *Cristal Nancy.* Identical to Bacc. #219 [1913]. Est. $400.00-$600.00.

COMMERCIAL PERFUME BOTTLES

Lot #156. Lanvin *Comme Ci Comme Ça* ceramic perfume bottle and stopper, 3.5" [8.9 cm], the bottom of the bottle with the label [name of the perfume], impressed *RL 7,* impressed with the Sevres mark, marked *Decoré a Sevres 1926.* Est. $5,000.00-$7,500.00.

Lot #157. Houbigant *Contraste* clear and frosted glass bottle and stopper, 3.5" [8.9 cm], near full and sealed. Est. $75.00-$125.00.

Lot #158. Elizabeth Arden *Splendor* clear glass bottle and stopper with atomizer underneath, 6" [15.2 cm], in its box. Est. $75.00-$150.00.

Lot #159. Lucien Lelong *French Lavender* frosted glass bottle molded with stars, 9.5" [24 cm], silver label around neck. Est. $100.00-$150.00.

Lot #160. Elizabeth Arden *5th Avenue* and frosted glass bottle and atomizer with 7.5" [19 cm], full of perfume, in its box. $75.00-$150.00.

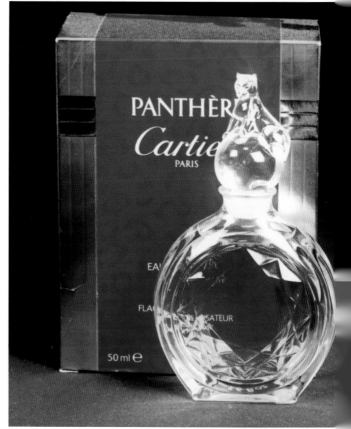

Lot #161. Lenthéric *Risque Tout* ['Risk it All'] clear glass bottle and stopper, 3" [7.6 cm], silver label at center, bottom signed *Lenthéric,* in its box. Est. $100.00-$150.00.

Lot #162. Cartier *Panthère* clear glass bottle and stopper, 4.7" [12 cm], per in the form of a panther, with perfume, bottom signed *Cartier,* in its and gold box. Est. $50.00-$100.00.

Lot #163. Parfums Salvador Dali *Le Roy Soleil* ['The Sun King'] clear and frosted glass bottle and stopper, 5.5" [14 cm], the bottle with atomizer, signed *Salvador Dali* in front, in its pink box. Est. $100.00-$200.00.

Lot #164. Jean Paul Gaultier *Summer Fragrance* clear glass bottle and metal atomizer attachment, 6.5" [16.5 cm], painted in multicolors with Tahitian design, in its metal can. Est. $50.00-$100.00.

Lot #165. Novaya Zarya ['New Dawn'] *Maska* ['Mask'] clear glass bottle and black cap, 4.1" [10.4 cm], gold label on bottom, with some of its perfume. Est. $50.00-$75.00.

Lot #166. Novaya Zarya ['New Dawn'] *Pikovaya Dama* ['Queen of Spades'] clear glass bottle and heart shaped stopper with long dauber, 3" [7.6 cm], the bottle molded with the queen on one side and hearts, diamonds and clubs on the other sides, in its box. Est. $150.00-$250.00.

Lot #167. Lucien Lelong *6* clear glass bottle and stopper; Worth *Je Reviens* frosted glass bottle and stopper, label at neck and blue glass bottle and brass cap; Chanel *No 5* clear glass bottle and stopper, in its box; Christian Dior *Diorissimo,* glass bottle with plastic cap; *Ombre Rose* black glass bottle with clear stopper; *No. 4711,* in its box. Seven items. Est. $100.00-$200.00.

Lot #168. Coty *Paris, Emeraude, L'Aimant, L'Origan* clear glass bottles with brass caps, 3.5" [8.9 cm], each with a gold label on front, in their clear plastic holder. Est. $100.00-$200.00.

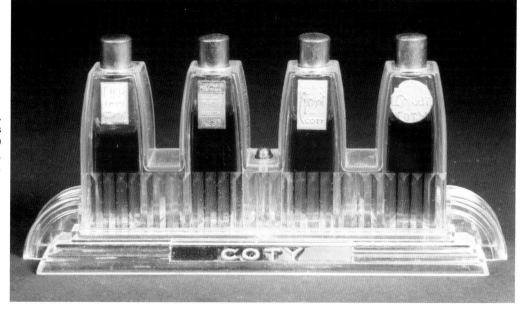

#169. Christian Lacroix clear glass bottle with atomizer attachment glass stopper, 4.7" [12 cm], shaped as a sea shell, in its red box. Est. 00-$100.00.

Lot #170. Jean Paul Gaultier *Fragile* clear glass atomizer ball and metal base, 4" [10.2 cm], the inside with a figure of a woman in black, in its box. Est. $75.00-$125.00.

#171. Bourjois *Ramage* ['Warbling'] clear glass bottle and gold 4.3" [11 cm], bottom with a factice label, gold label on front with a xeet motif, in its pretty gray box. This Bourjois fragrance from the 's is somewhat rare. Est. $150.00-$200.00.

Lot #172. Coty *L'Aimant* clear glass bottle and red stained frosted stopper, 3.4" [8.6 cm], full and sealed, label on front, in its smart red box. Est. $150.00-$250.00.

Lot #173. Matchabelli *Windsong* clear glass bottle and stopper completely enameled in green and gold, 3.4" [8.6 cm], bottom marked *Prince Matchabelli* in the mold; identical smaller bottle, 2.2" [5.6 cm], label on the bottom; identical smaller bottle, sealed, in plastic box. Three Items. Est. $200.00-$300.00.

Lot #174. Jean Patou *1000* clear glass bottle and stopper, 3.2" [8.1 cm], decorated in gold, empty, in its box; empty box for a much smaller bottle; Jean Patou *Joy* clear glass bottle and stopper, 2.6" [6.6 cm]; Ciro *Reflexions* clear glass bottle and stopper, 3.5" [8.9 cm]; boxes for Ciro *Les Pois de Senteur de Chez Moi* and Guerlain *L'Heure Bleue.* Six items. Est. $100.00-$200.00.

Lot #175. Lazell *Bocadia* clear glass bottle and stopper with black enamel, 3.9" [9.9 cm], unopened but with little perfume, gold label on front, in its colorful silk-lined box. Est. $100.00-$175.00.

Lot #176. Windsor House *Romeo and Juliet* [Parfum pour la Grande Occasion] clear glass bottles and plastic caps, 3.4" [8.6 cm], shaped as binoculars, with perfume, labels on bottle, in their box missing the bottom part. Est. $100.00-$200.00.

Lot #177. Lolita Lempicka light violet glass bottle and gold metal stopper, 3.5" [8.9 cm], shaped as an apple, the bottle enameled with leaves in white and gold, in a metal holder with ladybug stickpin, in its pretty box. Est. $100.00-$200.00.

Lot #178. Dana *Voodoo* clear glass bottle and black plastic cap, 3.5" [8.9 cm], full of perfume, on its metal plinth and in its black box. Est. $100.00-$200.00.

Lot #179. Elizabeth Arden *The Treasures of the Pharaohs* soapdish shaped with antilope heads on both sides, 10" long [25 cm], bottom signed *Elizabeth Arden* and *Made in Japan.* Est. $75.00-$125.00.

Lot #180. Prince Matchabelli *Potpourri Gypsy Patteran* clear glass bottle with corklined frosted stopper, label on bottom, empty, in its tambourine shaped box which says: "Where my Caravan has rested flowers I leave you on the grass." Est. $100.00-$150.00.

Lot #181. Caron *Infini* clear glass bottle and stopper of clear plastic that is a mirror image of the glass bottle, 4.4" [11.2 cm], label in black on front, full and sealed, in its box. Est. $150.00-$250.00.

Lot #182. Guerlain *Heliotrope Blanc* clear glass bottle and stopper, 3.9" [9.9 cm], near empty, bottom with Guerlain label and signed *Guerlain*. Est. $100.00-$200.00.

Lot #183. Elizabeth Arden *The Treasures of the Pharaohs* porcelain box molded as a cat, 7" [17.8 cm], decorated with Egyptian motifs, bottom signed *Elizabelth Arden Japan*. Est. $100.00-$200.00.

Lot #184. Fabergé *Tigress* Bedtime perfume frosted glass bottle and stopper, 4.2" [10.7 cm], decorated in a gold pattern, empty, bottom signed *Fabergé*, in its box. Est. $75.00-$150.00.

Lot #185. Guerlain *Vol de Nuit* dark olive green glass bottle and stopper, 3.5" [8.9 cm], the cap covered brass impressed *Guerlain*, the bottle molded with rays emanating from the center, brass medallion, empty, in its zebra motif box. Est. $200.00-$300.00.

Lot #186. Richard Hudnut *Green Rose* clear glass bottle and stopper, 3.4" [8.6 cm], pretty gold label on the front, in its dark green box. Est. $150.00-$250.00.

Lot #187. Niki de Saint Phalle *Eau de Toillette* blue glass bottle with atomizer attachment and metal cap with intertwined snakes, 3.7" [9.3 cm]; *Lait Satiné* blue glass bottle and metal cap, the front of the bottle painted with colorful snakes, empty. Two items. Est. $100.00-$200.00.

Lot #188. Niki de Saint Phalle *First Edition* blue glass bottle with gold metal stopper and two snakes intertwined, 3" [7.6 cm], bottom with label, in its elegant box of red and blue. Est. $200.00-$300.00.

Lot #189. Caron *Nocturnes* clear glass bottle encased in black plastic with clear glass stopper, 3.2" [8.1 cm], full of perfume, in its box with an abstract painting. Est. $150.00-$250.00.

Lot #190. Coty *Paris* clear glass bottle and stopper, 3.5" [8.9 cm], gold label at center, bottom signed *Coty,* in its pretty box. Est. $100.00-$200.00.

Lot #191. Escada *Acte 2* clear glass bottle and stopper, 4" [10.2 cm], with perfume, in its bright yellow box. Est. $50.00-$100.00.

Lot #192. Fabergé *Fleurs du Monde* clear glass bottle and amber glass top, 2.2" [5.6 cm], label around neck, full and sealed, in its box. Est. $100.00-$200.00.

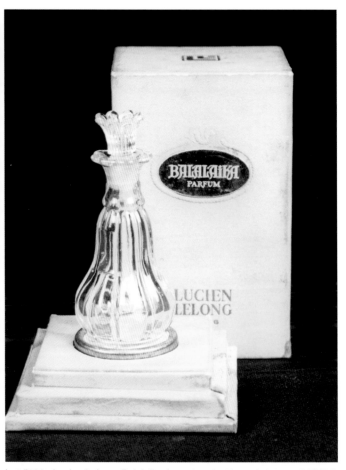

Lot #193. Lucien Lelong *Balalaika* clear glass bottle and stopper, 2.7" [6.8 cm], an unusual little bottle, label on bottom, in its box. Est. $150.00-$250.00.

Lot #194. Coty *L'Origan* clear glass bottle with inner stopper and brass overcap, 3.4" [8.6 cm], full and sealed, label at center, in its original box. Est. $200.00-$300.00.

Lot #195. Matchabelli *Beloved* clear glass bottle and stopper enameled in blue and gold in the shape of a crown, 2.2" [5.6 cm], full and sealed, gold label on bottom; *Princess Marie* white glass bottle and stopper in the shape of a crown, empty, label on bottom. Est. $200.00-$300.00.

Lot #196. Matchabelli *Beloved* clear glass bottle and stopper covered in blue and gold enamel, 2.2" [5.4 cm], full and sealed, in its original box [not shown]; *Ave Maria* clear glass bottle with gold enamel, 2.1" [5.1 cm], label on bottom. Est. $200.00-$250.00.

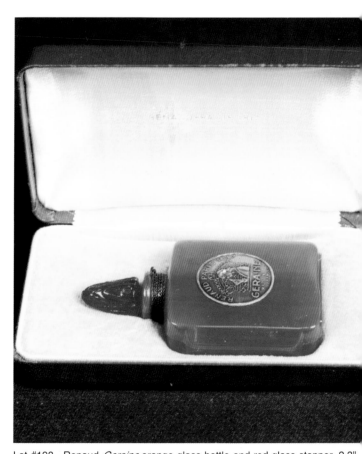

Lot #197. Matchabelli *Duchess of York* clear glass bottle and stopper, 3.4" [8.6 cm], decorated in gold enamel, bottom with labels and signed *Prince Matchabelli* in the mold. Est. $200.00-$300.00.

Lot #198. Renaud *Geraine* orange glass bottle and red glass stopper, 2.3" [5.8 cm], in its blue fitted case. Est. $200.00-$300.00.

Lot #199. Karl Lagerfeld *Sun Moon and Stars* blue glass bottle and metal stopper, 3.5" [8.9 cm], molded with the sun, moon and stars on the bottle, signed *Karl Lagerfeld* in gold, with its label; this is bottle 455 of an edition of 1200. This bottle was designed by IPBA member Susan Wacker. Est. $200.00-$300.00.

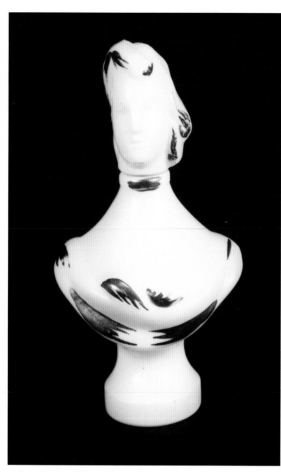

Lot #200. Gilbert Orcel *Coup de Chapeau* white glass bottle, inner stopper and overcap, 5" [12.5 cm], as the bust of a woman, highlights enameled in gold, empty, molded *Orcel Made in France*. Est. $250.00-$350.00.

Lot #201. Adorable Russian perfume bottle with a stopper of two horses heads [both grinning], 5.5" [14 cm]. marks from the Lomonosov factory, Imperial porcelain. Est. $600.00-$750.00.

Lot #202. Lucien Lelong *Eau de Cologne*, 6 [16.5 cm], stopper signed *Lucien Lelong;* t bottle is from the Century of Progress exh tion in Chicago. Est. $200.00-$300.00.

Lot #203. Matchabelli *Duchess of York* red glass bottle with gold stopper, 3.6" [9.1 cm], gold labels at the center and bottom of the bottle, bottom signed *Prince Matchabelli France*. Est. $300.00-$400.00.

Lot #204. Mary Chess *White Lilac* clear glass bottle and stopper, 3" [7.6 cm], in the shape of a chess castle, empty, names in white at base, in its box. Est. $150.00-$250.00.

Lot #205. Grenoville *Chaine d'Or* clear glass bottle and frosted cap, 3.4" [8.6 cm], label on front, the box decorated with Art Deco flowers and a tassel. Est. $100.00-$150.00.

Lot #206. Lenthéric *Pink Party* clear glass bottle and frosted glass stopper, 3.2" [8.2 cm], the bottle molded with flowers, pink label at the center, in its box topped with flowers. Est. $150.00-$250.00.

Lot #207. Schiaparelli *Snuff* clear glass bottle and plastic stopper, 5.2" [13.2 cm], full and sealed, label on front, bottom signed *Schiaparelli,* in its box. Est. $100.00-$200.00.

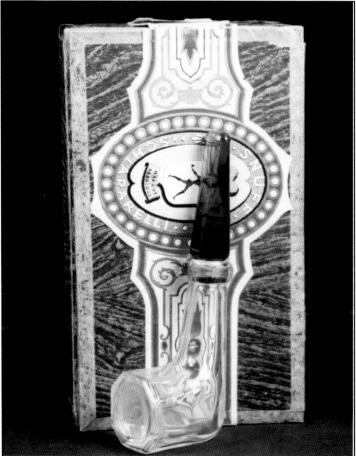

Lot #208. Schiaparelli *Snuff* clear glass bottle and amber glass stopper in the form of a pipe, 5.4" long [13.7 cm], empty, in its original box designed as if for cigars. Est. $400.00-$600.00.

Lot #209. Lucien Lelong *Ting-a-Ling Taglio* clear glass bottle and gold screw on stopper, 2" [5.1 cm], mounted with six bells all around it, with its labels front and bottom, in its box. Est. $200.00-$300.00.

Lot #210. Lucien Lelong *Parfum J* clear glass bottle and gold screw on stopper, 2.5" [6.4 cm], in its box with atomizer attachment. Est. $300.00-$500.00.

Lot #211. Coty *Asuma* frosted glass bottle and stopper, 2.7" [6.9 cm], decorated with flowers and leaves, empty, bottom signed *Coty France*, in its gold and Chinese red box decorated with oriental motifs. Est. $400.00-$600.00.

Lot #212. Lenthéric *Adam's Rib* clear glass bottle and stopper, 3.3" [8.4 cm], the bottle concave on the back side, gold "rib" stopper, names in gold on front, full and sealed, in its very pretty green box. Est. $150.00-$250.00.

Lot #213. Lucien Lelong *Parfum N* clear glass bottle and stopper, 4" [10.2 cm], of urn form, full and sealed, in its brown box. Est. $200.00-$300.00.

Lot #214. Lenthéric *A Bientôt* clear glass bottle with inner stopper and overcap, 2.1" [5.3 cm], full and sealed, in its box. Est. $200.00-$300.00.

Lot #215. Ciro *Ricochet* clear glass bottle and frosted glass stopper, 4" [10.2 cm], gold label at the neck and name in gold on the front, in its mint condition box. Est. $250.00-$350.00.

Lot #216. Saravel *Sables and Pearls* clear glass bottle, gold cap, and chrome overcap, 1.3" square [3.3 cm], *Saravel* molded on bottle, name on the chrome overcap, in bright pink satin box. Est. $200.00-$300.00.

Lot #217. Jean Patou *Moment Supreme* clear glass bottle and stopper, 4.5" [11.4 cm], full and sealed, label on the front, bottom signed *Jean Patou France*. Est. $100.00-$200.00.

Lot #218. Dana *Platinum* clear glass bottle and stopper, 2.6" [6.6 cm], labels at top of bottle and on bottom, full and sealed, in its very plush box. Est. $100.00-$200.00.

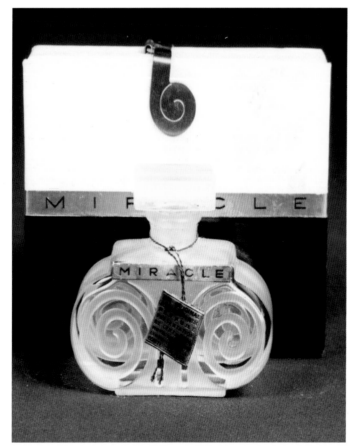

Lot #219. Lenthéric *Miracle* clear and frosted glass bottle and stopper, 2" [5.1 cm], an Art Deco design with a symmetrical swirl motif, empty, labels front and back, and on bottom. Est. $150.00-$250.00.

Lot #220. Coty *Paris* clear glass bottle and frosted glass stopper showing two butterflies, 3.2" [8.1 cm], the stopper with blue staining, in its original box and outer box. Est. $300.00-$500.00.

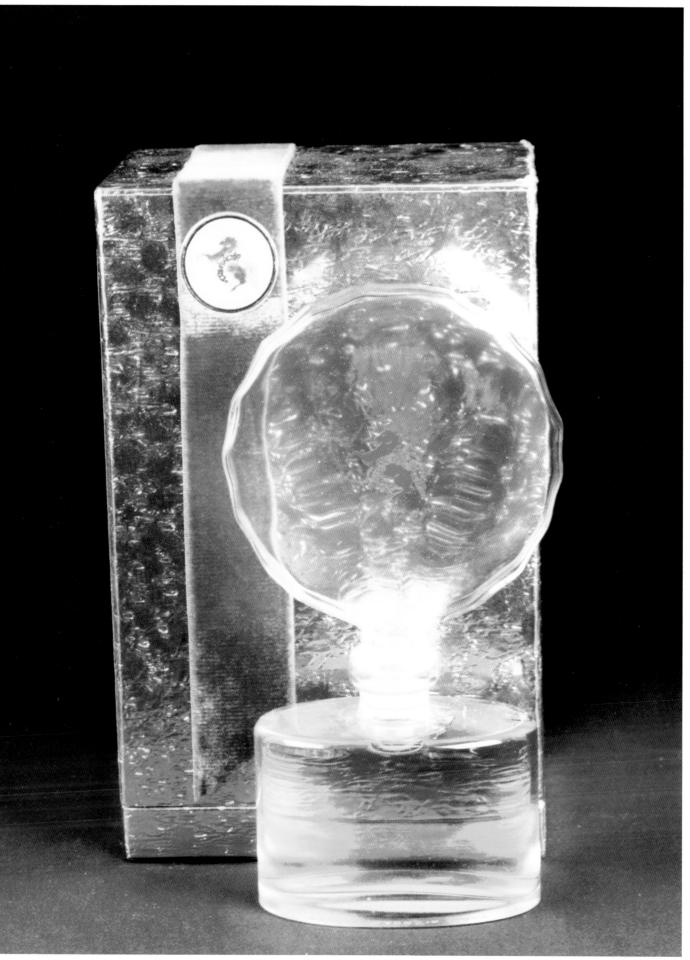

Lot #221. Elizabeth Arden *Blue Grass Flower Mist* oval bottle with enormous round stopper with the horse covered with flowers at center, 7.4" [18.8 cm], label on bottom, full and sealed, in its very pretty box. Est. $500.00-$750.00.

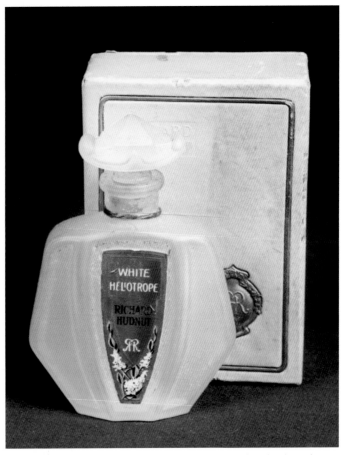

Lot #222. Richard Hudnut *White Heliotrope* frosted glass bottle and stopper, 3.4" [8.6 cm], label at the center, empty, in its original box. Est. $100.00-$200.00.

Lot #223. Fabergé *Woodhue* clear glass bottle and stopper, 3.9" [10 cm], label around neck, marked *Fabergé* in gold on the stopper, unopened, in its leather case with gold fleurs de lys, and box. Est. $100.00-$175.00.

Lot #224. Helena Rubenstein *Town* clear glass bottle and stopper, 3.3" [8.4 cm], names in black enamel on the front, empty, in its original box. Est. $300.00-$500.00.

Lot #225. Ciro *Gardenia Sauvage* clear glass bottle and stopper, 3.7" [9.4 cm], empty, green label at center, in its green box. Est. $200.00-$300.00.

Lot #226. Richard Hudnut *Extreme Violet* clear glass bottle and stopper, 4.5" [11.4 cm], full and sealed, bottom marked *Richard Hudnut,* in its original box decorated with the Russian double eagle. Est. $300.00-$500.00.

Lot #227. Richard Hudnut *Dubarry* clear glass bottle and stopper, 4.2" [10.6 cm], beautiful label, empty, with 8 1/8 cents of US Proprietary stamps marked *Hudnut December 1914.* Est. $300.00-$500.00.

Lot #228. Dana *Ambush* clear glass bottle and stopper, 3.1" [7.8 cm], unopened but perfume evaporated, label around the top, in its box. Est. $100.00-$200.00.

Lot #229. Weil *Cassandra* clear glass bottle and stopper, 3.6" [9.2 cm], in the shape of a classical column, full and sealed with wax, tied with small gold label, in its original box. Est. $400.00-$600.00.

Lot #230. Schiaparelli *Salut* clear glass bottle and stopper, 4.4" [11.2 cm], of rectangular form, not in pink but in navy blue, empty, bottom signed *Schiaparelli*. Est. $200.00-$300.00.

Lot #231. Lucien Lelong *Indiscret* cologne clear glass bottle and pink cap, 7.7" [19.5 cm], full and sealed, in its pretty box marked *Remembrances de Versailles*. Est. $100.00-$200.00.

Lot #232. Schiaparelli *Sleeping*, 7.5" [19 cm], signed *Schiaparelli*, in its box. Est. $200.00-$300.00.

Lot #233. Coty *Complice* ['Accomplice'] clear glass bottle and frosted glass stopper, 3.4" [8.6 cm], the stopper molded as a flower in tiara form, full and sealed, with advertising pamphlet, in its original box. Est. $200.00-$400.00.

Lot #234. Coty *Paris* clear glass bottle and frosted glass stopper, 3.6" [9.1 cm], label on the side, empty, in its beautiful box with tassel showing the names of perfume and company in fireworks. Est. $300.00-$400.00.

Lot #235. Elizabeth Arden *Memoire Chérie* frosted glass bottle and stopper shaped as a woman, 3.8" [9.6 cm], the stopper is the woman's head, empty. Est. $500.00-$750.00.

Lot #236. Vigny *Le Golliwogg* clear glass bottle and black glass stopper molded as a Golliwogg, 3.5" to top of hair [8.9 cm], bottom signed *Vigny* in the mold. Est. $150.00-$250.00.

Lot #237. Isadora clear glass bottle and frosted glass stopper as a kneeling woman, 4.5" [11.4 cm], full and sealed, marked *Isadora 1979*. Est. $100.00-$200.00.

Lot #238. Jeanne Lanvin clear glass bottle and gold stopper, 2.2" [5.5 cm], with the Lanvin logo in gold and the words *Jeanne Lanvin* just below it. Est. $150.00-$250.00.

Lot #239. Vantine's unknown perfume clear glass bottle and frosted glass stopper, 2.9" [7.4 cm], shaped as a buddha, empty, signed *Vantine's France*. Est. $500.00-$750.00.

Lot #240. Matchabelli *Damas* an unusual clear glass bottle and stopper, 3.5" [8.9 cm], the stopper with a crown and an *M,* full and sealed, label on bottom and on front. Est. $300.00-$500.00.

Lot #241. Lentheric *Anticipation* clear glass bottle and glass stopper with a metal overcap, 2.6" [6.6 cm], labels on the front and bottom of the bottle, with perfume and sealed. Est. $100.00-$200.00.

Lot #242. Chevalier Garde *Fleur de Perse* clear and frosted glass bottle and stopper, 2.3" [5.8 cm], designed as the Russian double eagle with a crown, label on bottom, in its box. Est. $400.00-$600.00.

Lot. #243. Dana *Bolero* clear glass bottle and black glass stopper, 3.5" [8.9 cm], gold label at front, in its box. Est. $200.00-$300.00.

Lot #244. Helena Rubenstein *White Flame* clear glass bottle and gold stopper, 5.5" [14 cm], names in white enamel, in its pretty purple box.
Est. $400.00-$600.00

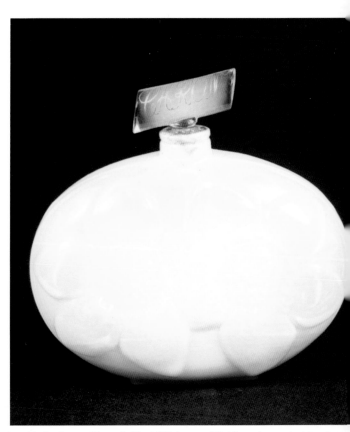

Lot #245. Lucien Lelong *Mon Image* clear glass bottle and stopper, 2.7" [6.8 cm], labels on front and back, in its beautiful mirrored box. Est. $300.00-$400.00.

Lot #246. Caron *Voeu de Noel* ['Christmas Wish'] opalescent white glass bottle and stopper, 3.6" [9.1 cm], empty, the front molded with a pair of open flowers, the stopper as a small bar, name in gold enamel on front, stopper signed *Caron* in gold. Est. $500.00-$750.00.

Lot #247. Schiaparelli *Shocking Body Radiance* clear glass bottle and stopper, 5.2" [13.2 cm], the front of the bottle with a painting signed *Dali*. Est. $500.00-$750.00.

Lot #248. Caron *Muguet de Bonheur* ['Lily of the Valley of Happiness'] clear glass bottle and stopper, 5.7" [14.5 cm], label on front, with a lily of the valley, full and sealed, in its mint condition box and outer box. Est. $300.00-$500.00.

Lot #249. Caron *Infini* clear glass bottle and stopper, 3.2" [8.1 cm], un-opened, with gold label on the front and also on the bottom, in its mint condition box. Est. $400.00-$600.00.

Lot #250. Houbigant *Présence* clear glass bottle and stopper, 3.5" [8.9 cm], an interesting bottle design, sealed but near empty, name in gold enamel on front, in its green box, with outer box. Ext. $400.00-$600.00.

Lot #251. Molinard *Xmas Bells* large black glass bottle and stopper, 4.2" [10.7 cm], in the form of a flattened bell, names in gold on front, empty, in its red and gold box. Est. $800.00-$1,200.00.

Lot #252. Matchabelli *Infanta Extract* clear glass bottle and stopper, 2.7" [6.8 cm], in the shape of an unusual Russian crown [*not* the usual model], full and sealed, label on bottom, in its beautiful fitted box. Est. $750.00-$1,000.00.

Lot #253. Ciro *Chevalier de la Nuit* clear glass bottle and stopper, 3.9" [9.9 cm], empty, red label on bottom, in its box. Est. $200.00-$300.00.

Lot #254. Matchabelli *Katherine the Great* clear glass bottle and gold stopper shaped as the Russian crown, 2.6" [6.6 cm], empty, label on bottom, in its box in red velvet and with white fur. Est. $300.00-$500.00.

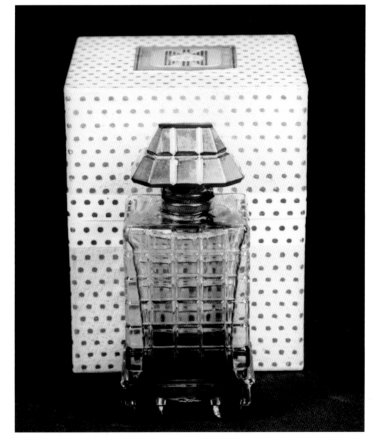

Lot #255. Caron *La Fête des Roses* ['Festival of Roses'] clear glass bottle and gold stopper, with a design of lines, label on bottom, some perfume, in its pink box. Est. $600.00-$800.00.

Lot #256. Lucien Lelong *Opening Night* clear glass bottle and stopper, 2.8" [7.1 cm], a pyramid shape, some perfume, labels on front and on bottom; it is *very* hard to find this bottle with the labels. Est. $500.00-$750.00.

Lot #257. Helena Rubenstein *Gala Performance* clear glass bottle and stopper, 6" [15.2 cm], in the shape of a dancer, label around neck, half full of perfume; this bottle is *much* rarer than the frequently seen bottle with the broad skirt. Est. $500.00-$750.00.

Lot #258. Rigaud *Féerie* ['Fairyland'] clear glass bottle and frosted glass stopper, 1.7" [4.3 cm], the stopper shaped as a flower, with its label, in its brown box. Est. $300.00-$400.00.

Lot #259. Lanvin *Arpege* black glass bottle and stopper, 5" [12.7 cm], *Lanvin* in gold on the side of the bottle, bottom inscribed *Lanvin*. Est. $100.00-$200.00.

Lot #260. Mary Chess *Souvenir d'un Soir* frosted glass bottle and stopper, 3.5" [8.9 cm], in the shape of the famous fountain outside the Plaza Hotel in New York City, full and sealed, in its elegant gold and black box. Est. $1,500.00-$2,500.00.

Lot #261. Hattie Carnegie *Perfume No. 7* clear glass bottle and stopper, 4.2" [10.7 cm], in the shape of a woman's head and shoulders, empty, the name molded in raised letters around the bottom of the bottle, in its seldom seen box with label on bottom. Est. $750.00-$1,250.00.

Lot #262. Schiaparelli *Si* clear glass bottle and stopper, 4.7" [12 cm], made to look like a bottle of wine, full and sealed, with its atomizer attachment, in its box and outer box. This one is quite rare, though we do not understand why. Est. $800.00-$1,200.00.

Lot #263. Coty *Emeraude* clear glass bottle and frosted glass stopper, 5.2" [13.2 cm], with perfume, label at center and on side, in its deluxe mirrored box. Est. $500.00-$750.00.

Lot #264. Coty *Ambre Antique* clear and frosted glass bottle and stopper, 6.2" [15.7 cm], the bottle a design of classical women in different poses, full and sealed, in its beautiful box marked *Edition 1995*. Est. $500.00-$750.00.

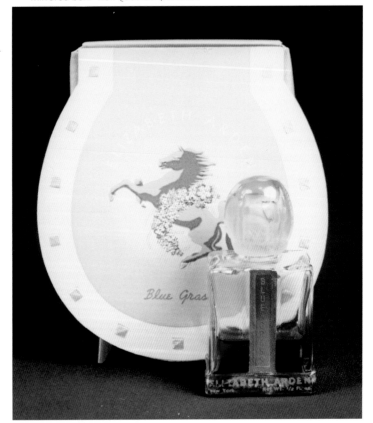

Lot #265. Elizabeth Arden *Blue Grass* clear glass bottle with inner stopper and turquoise blue overcap, 2.8" [7.1 cm], sealed with some perfume, bottom marked *Arden,* in its pretty box. Est. $500.00-$750.00.

Lot #266. Lenthéric *Asphodèle* rare clear glass bottle and black glass stopper, 4.5" [11.4 cm], a combination of sphere and pyramid, full and sealed with label at the neck, in its original tasseled box. Est. $500.00-$750.00.

Lot #267. Corday *Zigane* clear glass bottle and stopper, 3.7" [9.4 cm], shaped as a violin, names in gold on the front, in its violin shaped pink box. Est. $300.00-$500.00.

Lot #268. Lucien Lelong unidentified scent blue glass bottle and metal stopper, 9.2" [23.4 cm], large and impressive, no label, marked around stopper *Lucien Lelong*. Est. $500.00-$750.00.

THE FRENCH MASTERS OF PERFUME BOTTLE DESIGN:
DÉPINOIX - JOLLIVET - LALIQUE - VIARD - GAILLARD

Lot #269. Jaytho *Méchant Mais Charmant* ['Naughty but Nice'] frosted glass bottle and stopper, 2.5" [6.4 cm], a bouquet of tulips, molded *Jaytho*, in its box. Utt #JT-1. This very small size is hard to find. Est. $500.00-$750.00.

Lot #270. Forvil *Chypre* clear glass bottle and stopper of diminutive size, 3" [7.6 cm], with garlands of flowers, empty, bottom signed *R. Lalique* in the mold, in its brass case signed *Forvil*. Utt #F-7. Est. $350.00-$500.00.

Lot #271. Nina Ricci *Coeur Joie* miniature clear glass bottle and stopper, 2.4" [6.1 cm], sealed, in its box, bottom signed *Lalique.* Est. $250.00-$350.00.

Lot #272. Nina Ricci *L'Air du Temps* clear glass bottle and frosted glass stopper in the shape of two doves in flight, 6.4" [16.2 cm], signed *Lalique France* near the bottom; this is a very large and difficult to find size. Est. $200.00-$300.00.

Lot #273. Worth *Imprudence Eau de Cologne* huge size blue glass bottle and stopper in the shape of the moon and stars, 9.5" [24 cm], square label at the center, some perfume, bottom signed *R. Lalique.* Est. $500.00-$750.00.

Lot #274. Houbigant *Le Temps des Lilas* ['Lilac Time'] clear glass bottle and stopper, 3.3" [8.4 cm], the oval shape decorated with a design of molded vertical lines and spirals in rows, names in enamel near base, with perfume, molded signature *R. Lalique.* Utt #H-2 [1922]. Est. $1,250.00-$1,750.00.

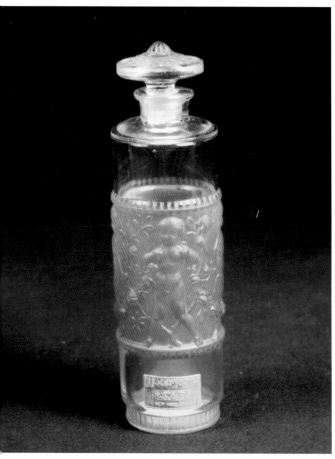

Lot #275. Woodworth *Tous Les Bouquets* ['All Flowers'] clear and frosted glass bottle and stopper, 5" [12.7 cm], the frosted parts with amber patina, label on front and bottom, signed *J. Viard.* Est. $1,500.00-$2,500.00.

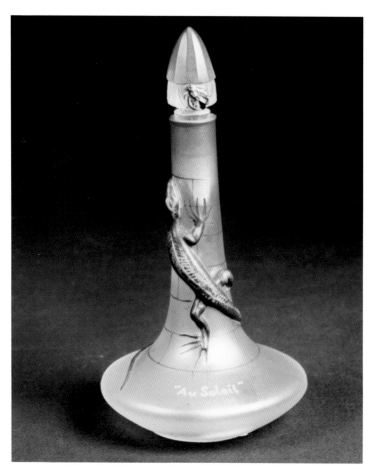

Lot #276. Lubin *Au Soleil* ['To the Sun'] frosted glass bottle and stopper, 5.6" [14.2 cm], enameled in dark green and gold with gray patina, empty, name in gold, bottom signed *Lubin Paris,* by M. Dépinoix, circa 1909-1912. Est. $2,500.00-$3,500.00.

Lot #277. Lucien Lelong *Parfum N* chrome box only [no bottle] in the skyscraper design, 4.6" [11.7 cm]; the box is for a bottle by René Lalique. Est. $500.00-$1,000.00.

Lot #278. Harriet Hubbard Ayer *Muguet* clear bottle and stopper, 3.7" [9.4 cm], bottom marked *France* and with the Harriet Hubbard Ayer monogram, with perfume, in its box. Est. $3,000.00-$4,000.00.

Lot #279. Forvil *Relief* clear glass bottle and stopper, 5.5" [14 cm], molded with a design of beads in spirals entirely covering both sides and stopper, bottom molded *R. Lalique.* This is the smaller of the three sizes of this model. Utt #F-8. Est. $1,000.00-$1,250.00.

Lot #280. Delettrez *Inalda* rare clear glass bottle and stopper, 3.6" [9. cm], the bottle formed by indented rows and decorated with dots in black enamel, cone shaped stopper also decorated with enamel dots, bottom molded *R. Lalique.* Utt #DEL-1. Est. $1,500.00-$2,000.00.

Lot #281. Maison Lalique *Telline* semi-opaque green glass bottle and stopper, 3.8" [9.7 cm], the bottle in the form of a large shell, the stopper molded as a smaller one, signed in the mold *R. Lalique;* this bottle in this color is quite rare. Utt #ML-508. Est. $4,000.00-$6,000.00.

Lot #282. Lucien Lelong *Étoile de Mer* ['Star of the Sea'] clear and frosted glass bottle and stopper, 4" [10.2 cm], the bottle an eight pointed star, label around neck, with its label, signed in the mold *R. Lalique.* Est. $1,000.00-$1,500.00.

Lot #283. Babani *Saigon* cobalt blue bottle and stopper, 3.4" [8.6 cm], decorated with birds in a berry tree, the bottom of the bottle with swirls of gold, marked around the neck *Babani Saigon Paris,* bottom of the bottle marked *Deposé Made in France.* Est. $1,000.00-$1,500.00.

Lot #284. Maison Lalique *Camille* rare dark blue glass bottle and stopper, 2.2" [5.5 cm], the highly sculptured design resembling that of a shell, etched signature *R. Lalique.* Utt #ML 516. Est. $4,000.00-$5,000.00.

Lot #285. Robj *Entre Tous* ['Just Between Us All'] extremely rare glass perfume bottle and stopper, 3.6" [9.1 cm], the design patinated in red, empty, with its label, in its very rare leather bound book-form box, containing a poem inside. Est. $3,000.00-$4,000.00.

Lot #286. Lalique *Limited Edition 2001 Mascotte Faune* ['Faun Mascot'] frosted glass bottle, 7" [17.8 cm], the stopper a replica of a Faun, full of cologne and with its atomizer attachment, in its original box with certificate of authenticity, signed *Lalique France.* Est. $800.00-$1,200.00.

Lot #287. Richard Hudnut *La Soirée* ['The Evening Party'] clear glass bottle and red glass stopper, 4.5" [11.4 cm], the bottle with a checkerboard pattern in diamonds, alternate rows colored red, empty, label in gold on the shoulder, in its beautiful quality red box. Est. $4,000.00-$6,000.00.

Lot #288. Small lapis lazuli crystal bottle, 2.4" [6.1 cm], molded as a basket bouquet of flowers, with its dauber, apparently unsigned. Est. $100.00-$200.00.

Lot #289. Clear crystal bottle with porcelain and metal overlay, 2" [5.1 cm], with porcelain medallion of a romantic couple, the top with a lady, signed *Czechoslovakia* on a metal tag around the neck. Est. $150.00-$250.00.

Lot #290. Miniature green crystal bottle and stopper, 2" [5.1 cm], rectangular bottle and round stopper, with its dauber, bottom signed *Czechoslovakia*. Est. $100.00-$200.00.

Lot #291. Miniature green crystal bottle and stopper, 3.4" [8.7 cm], decorated with metalwork and a green jewel, with its dauber, bottom signed *Czechoslovakia*. Est. $200.00-$300.00.

Lot #292. Small blue crystal bottle and stopper, 3.2" [8.1 cm], cut with an incised pattern, with its dauber, apparently unsigned. Est. $150.00-$250.00.

Lot #293. Green crystal bottle and clear crystal stopper, 3.3" [8.3 cm], the wreath stopper intaglio cut with flowers, dauber lacking, apparently unsigned. Est. $100.00-$150.00.

Lot #294. Clear crystal bottle and stopper, 5.6" [14.2 cm], the stopper cut as a prism, with its dauber, the bottom with Irice label and marked *Czechoslovakia*. Est. $100.00-$200.00.

Lot #295. Small clear bottle and stopper, 3.7" [9.4 cm], with its dauber, bottom signed *Czechoslovakia*. Est. $100.00-$200.00.

Lot #296. Violet crystal bottle and stopper, 5.4" [13.7 cm], asymmetrially cut, with its dauber, bottom signed *Czechoslovakia*. Est. $100.00-$200.00.

Lot #297. Blue crystal bottle and clear crystal stopper, 3.8" [9.6 cm], the bottle highly cut, the stopper an open circle, with its dauber, bottom signed *Czechoslovakia*. Est. $250.00-$350.00.

Lot #298. Clear crystal bottle and pink crystal stopper, 4.6" [11.6 cm], the bottle of octagonal shape, the stopper intaglio cut with an abstract design, with its tiny dauber, bottom signed *Czechoslovakia*. Est. $200.00-$300.00.

Lot #299. Adorable clear crystal bottle and blue crystal stopper, 3.7" [9.3 cm], the stopper intaglio cut with a maiden smelling flowers, with its tiny dauber, possibly unsigned. Est. $100.00-$150.00.

Lot #300. Deep yellow crystal bottle and clear crystal stopper, 5.9" [15 cm], the stopper partially cut out, with its dauber, with original label from Aristo, bottom signed *Czechoslovakia*. Est. $300.00-$500.00.

Lot #301. Yellow crystal bottle and clear crystal top, 6" [15.2 cm], both bottle and stopper elaborately cut, bottom signed *Czechoslovakia*. Est. $150.00-$250.00.

Lot #302. Large yellow crystal bottle and stopper, 6" [15.2 cm], elaborately cut in a geometric design, apparently unsigned. Est. $350.00-$450.00.

Lot #303. Yellow crystal bottle and stopper, 4.5" [11.4 cm], of simple geometric design with three bars cut into the stopper and on both sides of the bottle, unsigned. Est. $100.00-$200.00.

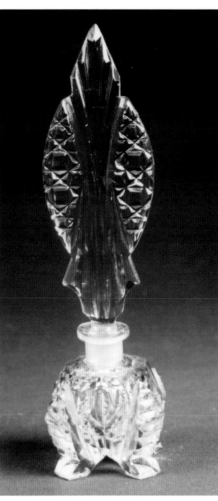

Lot #304. Blue crystal bottle and stopper, 5" [12.7 cm], both bottle and stopper decorated with flowers, dauber lacking, bottom signed *Czechoslovakia*. Est. $150.00-$250.00.

Lot #305. Peach crystal bottle and stopper, 7" [17.8 cm], dauber lacking, signed *Czechoslovakia,* and label of Premier. Est. $150.00-$250.00.

Lot #306. Blue crystal bottle and stopper, 5.5" [14 cm], the bottle intaglio cut with a ballerina and with original label on the bottom, signed *Czechoslovakia*. Est. $300.00-$400.00.

Lot #307. Pair of identical bottles of blue crystal bases with clear stoppers, 5" [12.7 cm], both bottles and stoppers cut with the same motif, the bottoms are cut but apparently unsigned. Est. $200.00-$300.00.

Lot #308. Blue crystal perfume bottle and clear stopper, 5.5" [14 cm], both bottle and stopper cut with a geometric pattern, with its dauber, bottom signed *Czechoslovakia*. Est. $200.00-$300.00.

Lot #309. Clear crystal bottle and pink stopper, 4" [10.2 cm], both bottle and stopper cut in reverse images of each other, with its dauber, bottom signed *Czechoslovakia*. Est. $200.00-$300.00.

Lot #310. Clear crystal bottle and stopper, 4.3" [10.9 cm], the stopper intaglio cut with a woman and her fan, dauber lacking, bottom signed *Czechoslovakia*. Est. $150.00-$250.00.

Lot #311. Clear crystal bottle and black crystal stopper, 5.2" [13.2 cm], cut on both sides with facets, with its dauber, bottom signed *Czechoslovakia*. Est. $150.00-$250.00.

Lot #312. Very rare set of four clear crystal bottles and black crystal stoppers on their black tray, tallest 3.2" [8.1 cm], all with daubers, bottom of each bottle signed *Czechoslovakia*. It is *extremely* rare to find a set such as this in such perfect condition. Est. $300.00-$500.00.

Lot #313. Clear crystal bottle and stopper, 4" [10.2 cm], the stopper intaglio cut with a goddess and two children, signed with the Hoffman butterfly; two small ashtrays with the same scene, and also with the Hoffman butterfly. Est. $300.00-$400.00.

Lot #314. Powder dish in clear and blue, 2.5" [6.4 cm], the top of the box with an unusual applied flower in blue, apparently unsigned. Est. $100.00-$200.00.

Lot #315. Clear crystal bottle and stopper, 5.1" [13 cm], intricately cut on both sides with geometric design, with its dauber, bottom signed *Czechoslovakia*. Est. $150.00-$250.00.

Lot #316. Clear crystal bottle and stopper, 5" [12.7 cm], highly cut all over with a geometric motif, with its dauber, bottom signed *Czechoslovakia*. Est. $150.00-$250.00.

Lot #317. Clear crystal bottle and very pale blue stopper, 5.3" [13.5 cm], bottle and stopper highly cut, stopper with an open part, with its dauber, bottom signed *Czechoslovakia*. Est. $150.00-$250.00.

Lot #318. Clear crystal bottle with red crystal stopper, 5.6" [14.2 cm], both bottle and stopper cut with a star motif, bottom signed *Czechoslovkia* and with the Irice label. Est. $150.00-$250.00.

Lot #319. Clear crystal bottle and red crystal stopper, 4.8" [12.2 cm], cut with abstract motifs, with its dauber, bottom with Irice paper label and signed *Czechoslovakia*. Est. $300.00-$500.00.

Lot #320. Clear crystal bottle and stopper, 6.4" [16.2 cm], the bottle and stopper identically cut with three panels, the stopper intaglio cut with flowers, dauber lacking, bottom signed *Czechoslovakia*. Est. $150.00-$250.00.

Lot #321. Miniature clear crystal bottle and violet crystal stopper, 2.9" [7.4 cm], both bottle and stopper highly cut, with its dauber, bottom signed *Czechoslovakia*. Est. $150.00-$250.00.

Lot #322. Pair of clear crystal bottles and stoppers, 5.6" [14.2 cm], the stoppers intaglio cut with a goddess, bottoms signed *Czechoslovakia* and one with original Morlee label. Est. $300.00-$400.00.

Lot #323. Peach crystal bottle and stopper, 6.6" [16.8 cm], the stopper highly cut and with a cut-out portion, the bottom with four feet and two enameled medallions, dauber lacking, bottom signed *Czechoslovakia*. Est. $300.00-$400.00.

Lot #324. Peach crystal bottle and stopper, 7.7" [19.5 cm], both bottle and stopper highly carved in a geometric pattern, bottom also carved, with its dauber, bottom apparently unsigned. Est. $400.00-$600.00.

Lot #325. Peach colored crystal bottle and stopper, 5.9" [15 cm], cut in the Art Deco fashion, with its dauber, bottom signed *Czechoslovakia*. Est. $300.00-$500.00.

Lot #326. Peach crystal bottle and clear crystal stopper, 3.7" [9.4 cm], the bottle beautifully covered with an opaque peach jewel and pearls, the stopper intaglio cut with a lady and wolfhound, the bottom with Morlee label and signed *Czechoslovkia*. Est. $500.00-$750.00.

Lot #327. Clear crystal bottle and stopper, 5" [12.7 cm], the bottle cut with a star motif on both sides, the stopper intaglio cut with Venus and Cupid, dauber lacking, bottom signed *Czechoslovakia*. Est. $150.00-$250.00.

Lot #328. Clear crystal bottle and stopper, 5.2" [13.2 cm], the stopper intaglio cut with a goddess and cupid, dauber lacking, bottom with partial label and signed *Czechoslovakia*. Est. $150.00-$250.00.

Lot #329. Clear crystal bottle and stopper, 4.6" [11.6 cm], the stopper intaglio cut with a little winged fairy and lily of the valley, with its dauber, bottom signed *Czechoslovakia*. Est. $400.00-$600.00.

Lot #330. Clear crystal bottle and stopper, 5.8" [14.7 cm], the stopper of a cherub amid flowers with a bird, the bottle highly cut, with its dauber, bottom with Morlee label and signed *Czechoslovakia*. Est. $300.00-$500.00.

Lot #331. Blue crystal bottle and stopper, 8.9" [22.6 cm], the stopper of tiara form and cut with intaglio flowers, with its dauber, bottom signed *Czechoslovakia*. Est. $600.00-$750.00.

Lot #332. Blue crystal bottle and stopper, 6.3" [16 cm], both bottle and stopper intaglio molded with the same flower, with its dauber, bottom signed *Czechoslovakia*. Est. $150.00-$250.00.

Lot #333. Blue crystal bottle and stopper, 6" [15.2 cm], cut all over with a geometric motif, with its dauber, apparently unsigned. Est. $150.00-$250.00.

Lot #334. Clear crystal bottle and blue crystal stopper, 4.7" [12 cm], the stopper intaglio cut with lovebirds on a branch with hearts, with its dauber, bottom signed *Czechoslovakia*. Est. $200.00-$300.00.

Lot #335. Clear crystal bottle and stopper, 6.3" [16 cm], the stopper intaglio cut with flowers and with a cut-out portion, dauber lacking, bottom signed *Czechoslovakia*. Est. $400.00-$600.00.

Lot #336. Huge size clear bottle and stopper, 8.6" [21.8 cm], the huge stopper features a frosted butterfly atop a stylized flower, dauber lacking, signed *Czechoslovakia* in an oval. Est. $500.00-$750.00.

Lot #337. Beautiful quality clear and frosted crystal bottle and stopper, 8.3" [21 cm], the stopper showing a man and woman in embrace, with cut-out portions, with its dauber, bottom apparently unsigned. Est. $750.00-$1,250.00.

Lot #338. Clear crystal bottle and stopper, 6.5" [16.5 cm], the stopper intaglio cut with an elaborate picture of a dancer in the Art Deco style highlighted with brown stain, with its dauber, bottom signed *Czechoslovakia*. Est. $500.00-$750.00.

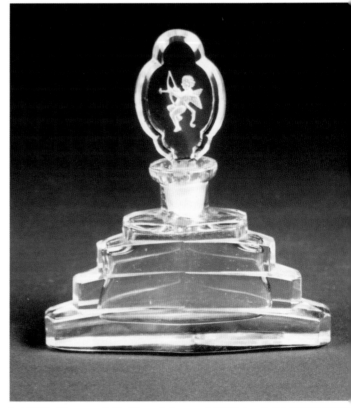

Lot #339. Clear crystal bottle and light blue crystal stopper, 4.7" [12 cm], the stopper intaglio cut with a bouquet of flowers, the stopper of tiara form, with its dauber, bottom signed *Czechoslovakia*. Est. $400.00-$600.00.

Lot #340. Clear crystal bottle and stopper, 4.5" [11.4 cm], the oblong bottle with four steps, the stopper with Cupid and his arrow, dauber lacking, bottom signed *Czechoslovakia*. Est. $100.00-$200.00.

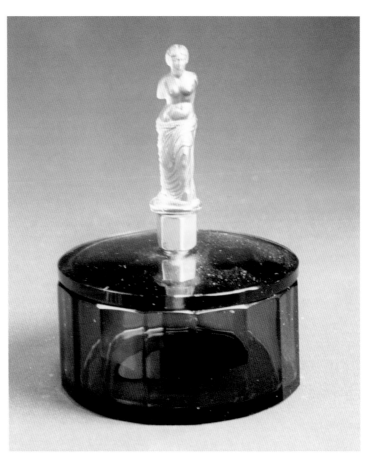

Lot #341. Violet crystal bottle and clear crystal stopper, 4.6" [11.7 cm], the bottle cut with three rows of lines in opposite directions, the stopper intaglio cut with lovebirds and hearts, with its dauber, bottom signed *Czechoslovakia*. Est. $300.00-$400.00.

Lot #342. Violet crystal box and cover with Venus de Milo, 5" [12.7 cm], apparently unsigned. Est. $750.00-$1,000.00.

Lot #343. Large violet crystal bottle and stopper, 6.5" [16.5 cm], the stopper a cresent moon, with its dauber, bottom signed *Czechoslovakia*. Est. $300.00-$500.00.

Lot #344. Violet colored crystal bottle and stopper, both bottle and stopper cut with an eight pointed star, with its dauber, bottom signed *Czechoslovakia*. Est. $200.00-$300.00.

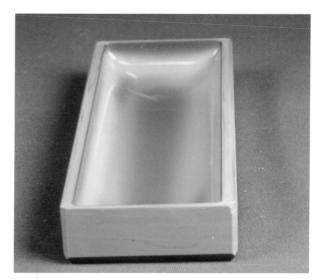

Lot #345. Rare lapis lazuli set of perfume bottle with nude in the grape leaves stopper, 7.5" [19 cm], covered box, and tray, impressed with a leaf design on the bottle and on the box, no dauber, bottom signed *Czechoslovakia* with paper label. Est. $1,250.00-$1,750.00.

Lot #346. Amber crystal bottle and stopper, 5.3" [13.5 cm], the entirety of the bottle covered with a metal frieze and amber jewels, dauber lacking, apparently unsigned. Est. $500.00-$750.00.

Lot #347. Beautiful quality dark green crystal bottle and stopper, 4.5" [11.4 cm], the base heavily encrusted with gold metalwork and green jewels, with its dauber, apparently unsigned. Est. $1,000.00-$1,500.00.

Lot #348. Black crystal bottle and stopper, 5" [12.7 cm], the fan shaped stopper carved with flowers, with its dauber, bottom signed *Czechoslovakia*. Est. $400.00-$600.00.

Lot #349. Opaque black crystal bottle and stopper, 7.6" [19.3 cm], the bottle molded on both sides with a nude, the stopper a simple black crystal, very rare gold highlights to the nude, with its dauber, completely unsigned. Est. $4,000.00-$6,000.00.

Lot #350. Black crystal bottle with a clear crystal stopper, 6.3" [16 cm], the stopper with an intaglio cut lady, flowers cut into the body of the bottle, with its long dauber, bottom signed *Czechoslovakia*. Est. $400.00-$600.00.

Lot #351. Black crystal bottle and clear crystal stopper, 5.5" [14 cm], the bottle molded with three steps, the stopper in the same shape as the bottle and intaglio cut with a dancer, with its dauber, bottom signed *Czechoslovakia*. Est. $250.00-$350.00.

Lot #352. Clear crystal bottle and stopper, 6.2" [15.7 cm], the stopper intaglio cut with a maiden holding a tray of flowers, with its dauber, bottom signed *Czechoslovakia*. Est. $250.00-$350.00.

Lot #353. Clear crystal bottle and stopper, 8" [20.3 cm], the stopper is beauti fully cut with a rose, the base enameled with a lady in a garden, with its dauber bottom faintly signed *Czechoslovakia*. Est. $400-00-$600.00.

Lot #354. Hoffman light smokey crystal bottle and stopper, 6.3" [16 cm], the bottle of simple faceted circular form, the stopper, with its dauber, featuring a classical maiden climbing uphill, signed with the Hoffman butterfly. Est. $1,000.00-$1,500.00.

Lot #355. [part of the lot; see description on next page.]

Lot #355. Extremely rare peach bottle and stopper with a standing dancer, powder jar, and atomizer bottle, 10.5" [26.7 cm], the dancer is nude from the waist upward, with its dauber, apparently unsigned. Est. $4,000.00-$6,000.00.

Lot #356. Black crystal bottle and clear crystal stopper in the shape of a butterfly, 2.7" [6.8 cm], the front of the bottle mounted with pearls and green stones, with its dauber, bottom signed *Czechoslovakia.* Est. $400.00-$600.00.

Lot #357. Beautiful Hoffman black crystal bottle and green crystal stopper, 4.2" [10.6 cm], the front of the bottle beautifully molded with Leda and the Swan, the stopper with a flying swan, with its green dauber, bottom signed with the Hoffman butterfly. The opaque black and malachite combination is very rare. Est. $2,500.00-$3,500.00.

Lot #358. Black crystal bottle and red crystal stopper, 5.8" [14.7 cm], the bottle painted in gold and silver with a boy playing the trumpet, with its long dauber, bottom signed *Czechoslovakia.* Est. $600.00-$750.00.

Lot #359. Black crystal bottle and red crystal stopper, 5" [12.7 cm], the bottle decorated with red stones, the stopper a hexagonal column, with its dauber, bottom signed *Czechoslovakia.* Est. $800.00-$1,000.00.

Lot #360. Red crystal bottle and clear crystal stopper, 5" [12.7 cm], the bottle a deep red, the stopper intaglio cut with a woman and child with flowers, with its dauber, bottom signed *Czechoslovakia* and with Silverleaf label. Est. $600.00-$800.00.

Lot #361. Red crystal bottle and stopper, 4.9" [7.4 cm], the bottle and the stopper cut with stars and an abstract motif, with its dauber, bottom signed *Czechoslovkia*. Est. $500.00-$750.00.

Lot. #362. Red crystal bottle and stopper, 4.8" [12.2 cm], the stopper cut with a nude on a ball, with its dauber, bottom signed *Czechoslovakia*. Est. $750.00-$1,000.00.

Lot #363. Red crystal bottle with clear figural stopper cut in the form of a bow, 4" [10.2 cm], the bottle cut on the diagonal forms two front-to-back cylindrical feet, an unusual brilliance to the crystal, with its dauber, bottom signed *Czechoslovakia*. Est. $1,000.00-$1,500.00.

Lot #364. Small clear crystal bottle and red crystal stopper, 3.2" [8.1 cm], both bottle and stopper beautifully cut with stars, with its dauber, bottom signed *Czechoslovakia*. Est. $300.00-$400.00.

Lot #365. Superb quality black crystal bottle and vaseline crystal stopper, 4.7" [11.9 cm], the bottle decorated with realistic glass fiery opal stones and pearls, the stopper showing a lady blowing bubbles with hearts inside and Cupid watching, stopper signed with the Hoffman butterfly. Est. $1,500.00-$2,000.00.

Lot #366. Vaseline crystal bottle and stopper, 4.3" [10.9 cm], the stopper intagio cut with a nude among branches, and with cut-out portions, signed with the Hoffman butterfly. Est. $400.00-$600.00.

Lot #367. Very large clear crystal bottle and stopper, 8.8" [22.3 cm], the stopper a cut prism, the bottle mounted with blue jewels, with its dauber, bottom signed *Czechoslovakia*. Est. $1,500.00-$2000.00.

Lot #368. Clear crystal bottle and stopper, 5.9" [15 cm], the bottle of octagonal form, both bottle and stopper cut with the same pattern, bottom with paper label and signed *Czechoslovakia*. Est. $200.00-$300.00.

Lot #369. Clear crystal bottle and stopper, 7" [17.8 cm], the stopper intaglio cut with a nude lady in a waterfall, with its dauber, bottom signed *Made in Czechoslovakia*. Est. $2,000.00-$2,500.00.

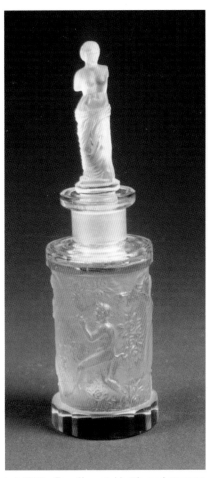

Lot #370. Peach crystal bottle and stopper, 6.5" [16.5 cm], the bottle with Pan the flute player and dancing draped nudes, the stopper as Venus de Milo, dauber lacking, signed *Czechoslovakia*. Est. $2,000.00-$2,500.00.

Lot #371. Gigantic rare size clear crystal bottle and stopper, 11.3" [28.7 cm], the stopper cut as a starburst, with its long dauber, bottom signed *Czechoslovakia*. Est. $500.00-$750.00.

Lot #372. Enormous blue crystal bottle and clear crystal stopper, 11" [28 cm], the stopper intaglio cut with a romantic couple, the base highly cut, with its dauber, bottom signed *Czechoslovakia*. Est. $1,500.00-$2,000.00.

Lot #373. Large malachite bottle and stopper, 5.4" [13.7 cm], the bottle molded with two faces in profile, the stopper molded with flowers, with its dauber, apparently unsigned. Est. $1,000.00-$1,500.00.

Lot #374. Clear crystal bottle and frosted glass stopper, 6" [15.2 cm], mounted on four feet, the stopper with two women and many cut-out portions, with its dauber, apparently unsigned. Est. $800.00-$1,200.00.

Lot #375. Pink crystal bottle and stopper, 5.6" [14.2 cm], the stopper with a lady dancing with garlands of flowers, with its dauber, bottom unsigned. This model is very rare. Est. $1,000.00-$1,500.00.

Lot #376. Large charcoal crystal bottle and stopper, 6.9" [17.5 cm], painted in gold with harp motifs and leaves on both bottle and stopper, acid etched mark but with much wear. Est. $300.00-$400.00.

Lot #377. Charcoal grey crystal bottle and clear crystal stopper, 6" [15.2 cm], the stopper cut with abstract motifs, the bottle cut with a maiden in a bonnet and dress, dauber lacking, bottom signed *Czechoslovakia.* Est. $150.00-$250.00.

Lot #378. Smoke crystal bottle with clear crystal stopper, 5.5" [14 cm], with its dauber, covered with metal filigree and an unusual Hoffman type glass medallion depicting a goddess with Cupid, bottom signed *Czechoslovakia* and also signed with a metal tag. Est. $750.00-$1,000.00.

Lot #379. Clear crystal bottle and stopper, 4.8" [12.2 cm], unusually made with parts of the bottle and stopper enameled black, small intaglio cut lady in the stopper, with its dauber, apparently unsigned. Est. $800.00-$1,200.00.

Lot #380. Unusual clear crystal bottle and metal atomizer top, 6.4" [16.3 cm], the bottle decorated with black enamel, on an elaborate metal holder, of Czechoslovakian manufacture. Est. $1,000.00-$1,500.00.

Lot #381. Clear crystal bottle and stopper, 7.8" [19.8 cm], the square bottle is highly cut, the stopper with Art Deco flowers, with its dauber, bottom signed *Czechoslovakia*. Est. $300.00-$500.00.

Lot #382. Clear crystal perfume bottle and stopper, 7.2" [18.3 cm], the stopper formed as a very large open loop, cut on both sides, bottom signed *Czechoslovakia*. Est. $400.00-$600.00.

Lot #383. Very rare alexandrite crystal bottle and stopper, 6.3" [16 cm], the bottle hexagonal, the stopper a lady reclining nude among grape leaves, dauber lacking, Ingrid label on the bottom. This bottle changes color under ultraviolet light from heather to periwinkle blue. Est. $2,500.00-$3,500.00.

Lot #384. Clear bottle with a pink nude dauber, 5.1" [13 cm], with a seldom seen original paper label documentation from Stix Baer & Fuller, St. Louis, as well as a paper label saying *Made in Czechoslovakia*. These are normally seen without any marks or documentation. Est. $2,500.00-$3,500.00.

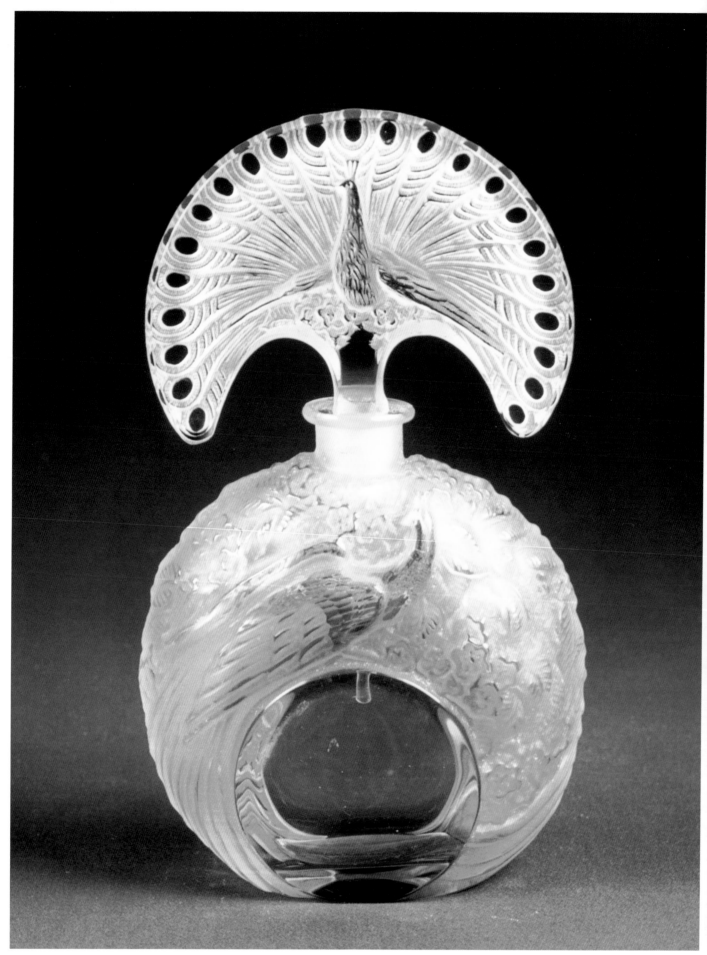

Lot #385. Sumptuous and rare set of two items: perfume bottle with a giant peacock whose feathers swoop around, 7.6" [19.3 cm], with its dauber; atomizer bottle [bulb lacking]; there are clear round parts to both items, apparently unsigned. Two items. Est. $2,000.00-$2,500.00.

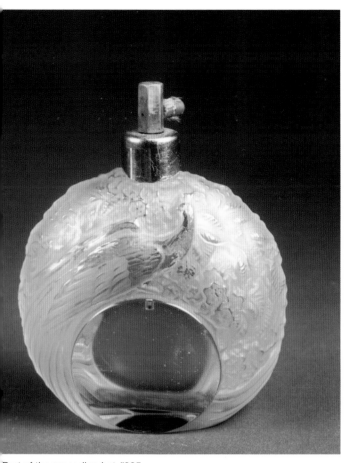

Part of the preceding Lot #385.

Lot #386. The powder jar ensuite to the preceding lot. It is very rarely seen. It is 4.8" [12.2 cm]. Est. $500.00-$1,000.00.

Lot #387. Pink colored crystal bottle and stopper, 5.5" [14 cm], covered with a frieze of jewels, the stopper intaglio cut with lilies of the valley, with its dauber, bottom faintly signed *Czechoslovakia*. Est. $1,250.00-$1,750.00.

Lot #388. Clear crystal bottle and pink crystal stopper, 7.5" [19 cm], the stopper a lady holding a bouquet of flowers, with cut-out portions, with its dauber, bottom signed *Czechoslovakia*. Est. $500.00-$750.00.

Lot #389. Translucent turquoise bottle and chrome metal stopper, 5.5" [14 cm], the stopper a fairy with a horn of plenty, bottom signed *Czechoslovakia* and the stopper signed *Austria*. Est. $300.00-$500.00.

Lot #390. Blue crystal bottle and clear crystal stopper, 6.7" [17 cm], the stopper a basket of flowers with cut-out portions, the bottle highly cut, with its dauber, bottom signed *Czechoslovakia*. Est. $500.00-$750.00.

Lot #391. Highly unusual clear crystal bottle and blue crystal stopper in the shape of a cube, 4.8" [12.2 cm], molded with an Art Deco motif and enameled blue, with its dauber, apparently unsigned. Est. $500.00-$750.00.

Lot #392. The bluebird of happiness: a rare clear crystal bottle and turquoise blue screw-on stopper in the shape of a bird, with its dauber, bottom signed *Czechoslovakia* and also signed on small tag. Est. $400.00-$600.00.

Lot #393. Beautiful turquoise blue crystal bottle and stopper, 6" [15.2 cm], the stopper molded with two dancers, the bottle molded with daffodils, dauber lacking, apparently unsigned. Est. $1,500.00-$2,000.00.

Lot #394. Violet crystal bottle and clear crystal stopper, 6.8" [17.3 cm], the stopper intaglio cut with a nymph with enormous wings smelling a flower, with its dauber, bottom signed *Czechoslovakia*. Est. $1,250.00-$1,750.00.

Lot #395. Elegant and desirable Ingrid bottle and stopper in very rare opa turquoise, 7.7" [19.5 cm], the front of the bottle with a nude sea nymph in re with its dauber, bottom with Czechoslovakian label. Est. $3,500.00-$4,50C

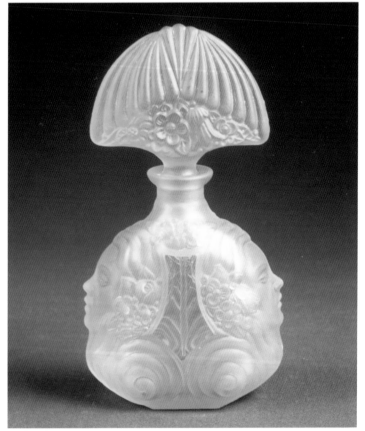

Lot #396. Brilliant translucent aqua crystal bottle and stopper, 6.4" [16.3 cm], molded with two heads on either side, the back of the bottle molded with flowers, clear panel at the center, with its dauber, bottom signed *Czecho-slovakia*. Translucent aqua is rare. Est. $1,500.00-$2,000.00.

Lot #397. Exceedingly rare box of amber crystal, 4.5" [11.4 cm], the box molded with the three muses atop each playing a different instrument, bottom apparently unsigned. The detailing on the faces and musical instruments is very fine. Est. $1,000.00-$1,500.00.

Lot #398. The Birth of Venus [from the foam of the sea], a very fine amber crystal bottle and stopper, 7" [17.8 cm], the bottle spherical and resting on three feet, its entire surface covered with a swirling mass of fish molded in relief, the stopper in the form of a shell in which the nude Venus kneels with a large strand of pearls, with its dauber, signed with a foil label, by Ingrid Made in Czechoslovakia. Est. $2,000.00-$3,000.00.

Lot #399. Blue crystal bottle and clear crystal stopper, 7" [17.8 cm], the stopper intaglio cut with flowers and asymmetrically cut, dauber lacking, bottom with original Paris Decorators label and signed *Czechoslovakia*. Est. $200.00-$300.00.

Lot #400. Clear crystal bottle and stopper, 5" [12.7 cm], the stopper with a kneeling lady intaglio cut, the base entirely covered with blue, green and amber stones front and back, possibly unsigned. Est. $1,000.00-$1,250.00.

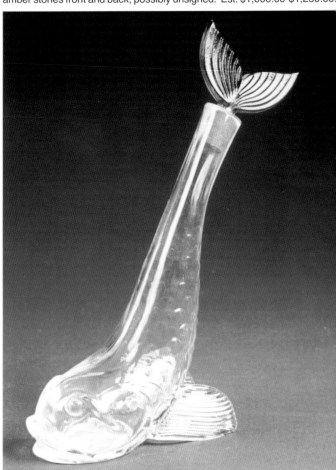

Lot #401. Yellow crystal bottle with clear crystal stopper, 6.2" [15.7 cm], the stopper molded with the harem dancer holding a tambourine, her foot going down into the bottle, with its dauber, bottom signed *Czechoslovakia*. Usually seen in pink or clear; yellow is rare. Est. $3,500.00-$4,500.00.

Lot #402. Clear glass bottle in the shape of a dolphin with a teal tail, 8" [20.3 cm], realistically molded, bottom signed with a paper label. Full figure three dimensional bottle and stopper combinations are quite rare. Est. $1,500.00-$2,000.00.

Lot #403. Pink crystal bottle and stopper, 7.5" [19 cm], the base with nine protruding feet, the stopper molded as a three dimensional nude holding up the world symbolized by an opaque crystal globe, with its dauber, bottom with paper label and signed *Czechoslovakia*. Est. $6,000.00-$7,500.00.

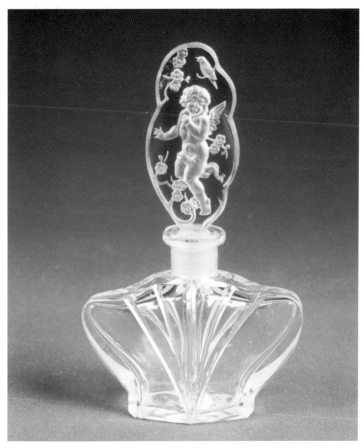

Lot #404. Yellow crystal bottle and stopper, 5.6" [14.2 cm], the stopper featuring a laughing child and a bird among flowering plants, with its dauber, apparently unsigned. Est. $350.00-$450.00.

Lot #405. Yellow crystal bottle and clear crystal stopper, 7.4" [18.8 cm], the stopper intaglio cut with two cupids standing on a flower, with its dauber, bottom signed *Czechoslovakia*. Est. $400.00-$600.00.

Lot #406. Purple frosted crystal bottle and stopper, 7" [17.8 cm], mounted with jewels on the front, the back with a window, completely covered with metalwork. Est. $1,500.00-$2,000.00.

Lot #407. Opaque black bottle and frosted glass pierced stopper with nude, 5.5" [14 cm], the stopper is signed with the Hoffman butterfly, the front of the bottle with a beautiful cameo of a woman's head. Est. $1,500.00-$2,500.00.

Lot #408. Heather crystal bottle and clear crystal stopper, 5.7" [14.5 cm], the stopper a lady playing the flute, with its dauber, bottom signed with Irice label Made in Czechoslovakia. Heather bottles are rarely seen. Est. $1,250.00-$1,750.00.

Lot #409. Spectacular clear crystal bottle with yellow crystal stopper, 5.8" [14.7 cm], the rare tiara stopper with a butterfly amid flowers, with cut-out portions in the crystal, signed *Czechoslovakia*. Est. $1,500.00-$2,000.00.

Lot #410. Clear crystal bottle and stopper, 5.2" [13.2 cm], the very rare stopper with two nudes done in the Lalique style, with its dauber, bottom signed *Czechoslovakia* and with partial Morlee label. Est. $2,000.00-$2,500.00.

Lot #411. Clear crystal bottle and stopper, 9.5" [24 cm], the stopper with cut out portions, the bottle on one side with flowers and on the other two lovers, with its dauber, bottom signed *Czechoslovakia*. Est. $2,000.00-$2,500.00.

Lot #412. Clear crystal bottle and blue crystal stopper, 6.9" [17.5 cm], the stopper intaglio cut with a lady and a peacock, with its dauber, bottom signed *Czechoslovakia*. Est. $500.00-$750.00.

Lot #413. Clear crystal bottle and blue crystal stopper, 7.3" [18.5 cm], the stopper intaglio cut with a woman picking flowers, with its dauber, bottom apparently unsigned. Est. $750.00-$1,250.00.

Lot #414. Superb quality pink crystal bottle and clear crystal stopper, 7.5" [19 cm], the bottle cut with sixteen protrustions, the stopper intaglio cut with three nudes (the three graces) cut into both sides of the stopper, one nude stained pink, one blue and one clear, dauber lacking, apparently unsigned. Est. $3,000.00-$3,500.00.

Lot #415. Beautiful botlle of clear and frosted crystal, 6.8" [17.3 cm], the unusual bottle molded on four sides with different nude women, the bottle with mauve stain on the frosted parts, with its long dauber, bottom signed *Ingrid Czechoslovakia*. Est. $5,000.00-$7,500.00.

Lot #416. Extremely rare malachite crystal bottle and stopper, 7.9" [20 cm], the bottle molded with a frieze of six classical very detailed nudes around the bottle supporting bowers of flowers, firebird stopper, dauber lacking, unsigned, by Ingrid. This bottle has exceptionally fine molding and detail.
Est. $3,000.00-$4,000.00.

Lot #417. Beautiful large malachite bottle and stopper, 8.5" [21.6 cm], beautifully decorated with four different panels, two with nudes and two with cupids, the elegant pierced stopper with a dancing nude and long malachite dauber [restored], stopper and bottle both signed with the Hoffman butterfly. This is the large version of this bottle and is exceedingly rare. Est. $2,500.00-$3,500.00.

Lot #418. Gorgeous and rare Ingrid opaque red bottle and stopper, 6.6" [16.7 cm], both bottle and stopper covered in bluebells in high relief, with its dauber, bottom signed *Czechoslovakia*. Est. $3,000.00-$4,000.00.

Lot #419. Red crystal bottle and clear crystal stopper, 6.5" [16.5 cm], the bottle molded on both sides with a nude and flowers, the stopper a bouquet of the same flowers with its dauber, apparently unsigned. Est. $5,000.00-$7,500.00.

Lot #420. Extremely rare pink bottle and stopper, 5.9" [15 cm], the unusual bottle cut somewhat like rays of the sun, the stopper a very rare sitting nude, legs tucked under her with her head back and face toward the sun, her hands demurely resting on her legs, with its dauber, signed *Ingrid,* made in Czechoslovakia. Est. $6,000.00-$7,500.00.